Men-at-Arms • 465

Brazilian Expeditionary Force in World War II

C.C. Maximiano & R. Bonalume N.
Illustrated by R. Bujeiro
Series editor Martin Windrow

First published in Great Britain in 2011 by Osprey Publishing,
PO Box 883, Oxford, OX1 9PL, UK
PO Box 3985, New York, NY 10185-3985, USA
Email: info@ospreypublishing.com

Osprey Publishing, part of Bloomsbury Publishing Plc.

Transferred to digital print on demand 2014

First published 2011
1st impression 2011

Printed and bound by Cadmus Communications, USA.

A CIP catalogue record for this book is available from the British Library.

ISBN: 978 1 84908 483 3

Editorial by Martin Windrow
Page layouts by Melissa Orrom Swan, Oxford
Index by Alison Worthington
Originated by United Graphics Pte
Typeset in Helvetica Neue and ITC New Baskerville

Artist's note

Readers may care to note that the original paintings from which the colour plates in this
book were prepared are available for private sale. All reproduction copyright whatsoever
is retained by the Publishers. All enquiries should be addressed to:

Ramiro Bujeiro, C.C. 28, 1602 Florida, Argentina

The Publishers regret that they can enter into no correspondence upon this matter.

The Woodland Trust

Osprey Publishing is supporting the Woodland Trust, the UK's leading woodland
conservation charity, by funding the dedication of trees.

www.ospreypublishing.com

BRAZILIAN EXPEDITIONARY FORCE IN WORLD WAR II

INTRODUCTION

World War II was a global conflict in the most profound sense of the word. Given its strategic position with a long coastline on the South Atlantic, and its reserves of strategic materials such as minerals and rubber, Brazil would inevitably find itself involved in the political and military events of the 1940s – it was simply a question of when, and how.

When President Washington Luís was overthrown in the revolution of 1930, Getúlio Vargas, a *caudillo* from the state of Rio Grande do Sul, interrupted a democratic process that had been initiated in the early decades of the 19th century. Vargas and the political leadership that he gathered around him attempted to modernize the country by means of a directed economy, abandoning what was considered by many to be a flawed democracy, and seizing both economic and political powers from the coffee-producer oligarchies that had previously ruled the country.

From the mid-1930s, US President Franklin D. Roosevelt showed concern for the safety of the Western Hemisphere. He was aware that Germany's speedy economic development would attract the attention of many governments in South and Central America, and the US followed the increasing German influence in countries like Brazil and Argentina with growing unease. The situation was considered alarming by some American policy-makers, particularly due to the large numbers of citizens of Italian origin living in the Brazilian state of São Paulo, others of German extraction in the southern states, and a large population of Japanese and their descendents – the least integrated of all immigrants in Brazilian society. It was feared that a population of such varied origins could be manipulated by the Axis to further their South American interests. Moreover, the radicalization of Vargas' regime following a *coup d'état* headed by the Army in 1937 was labeled as "fascist" by the American press.

The commercial ties between Brazil and the Axis were another source of worry for the United States. Seeking military, industrial, and economic development, Brazil was preoccupied by perceived threats to its southern border, and a continental rivalry with Argentina had been a traditional

Inscribed in August 1945, this portrait photo shows a private named Costa. He wears an unmodified example of the summer twill combat shirt, complete with his decorations and an Italian-made 1st Expeditionary Infantry Division shoulder patch. The three white bars below it indicate nine months' overseas service. (Julio do Valle)

characteristic of regional relations. Germany and Italy both pursued a policy of offering to exchange the up-to-date military hardware Brazil needed to ensure its defense for Brazilian raw materials. The US could not allow Brazil to become an exclusive market for the Germans and Italians; realizing – unsurprisingly – that he could profit from this competitive context, President Vargas began negotiating with the Americans for the establishment of a steel-mill complex in Volta Redonda. As the 1940s approached, however, Brazil's leeway for playing off the Axis and the US against one another became narrower. Dealings with the latter became closer and deeper – a natural consequence of the fact that Brazil was mainly under the hemispheric strategic influence of America, rather than any tribute to Vargas' political shrewdness.

Pvt José Marino, 5th Infantry Regiment, photographed in 1943 prior to his transfer to an expeditionary unit. He wears the M1934 tunic and cap in two shades of olive green; his cap badge shows crossed rifles and a grenade, above "5," indicating his branch and unit. (J. Marino)

The Brazilian armed forces in the interwar period

Before World War II the Brazilian armed forces were obsolete, and faced the challenge of rapid modernization if they were to become fit for any participation in the coming world conflict.

The Navy had two "dreadnought" battleships built in Great Britain in 1910, and only one of them had been barely modernized. Nevertheless, the Navy's very small cruisers would be useful as antisubmarine vessels, as would some Brazilian-built minelayers converted to that role.

The Army presented a mixture of French doctrine with weapons of several different origins. In the early decades of the 20th century the Brazilian Army, like most South American armies, pursued a quest for both intellectual and material modernization, and from 1921 onwards a French military mission was hired to instill its doctrine throughout the army. (The test of combat in Italy in 1944–45 would reveal inadequacies in the quality of this training, and in the absorption of modern European doctrine through the ranks of the Brazilian officer corps, particularly at senior level.) In the late 1930s a major arms deal with Germany, in return for the furnishing of raw materials, was intended to provide a considerable boost in equipment, especially in artillery, but the outbreak of war in 1939 prevented the delivery of more than a small proportion of what had been ordered. The Army's arsenal presented a motley picture, including US Colt pistols and Smith & Wesson revolvers, German Mauser rifles, Czech automatic rifles, French mortars and 75mm howitzers, and Italian tankettes.

The Air Force was created in 1941 by merging the former Navy and Army air arms. It inherited 99 aircraft from the Navy, including 36 Focke-Wulf Fw 44J Stieglitz biplane trainers, and 16 Fw 58B Weihe bombers. The Army contributed 331 aircraft of a staggering 25 different models, including 30 North American NA-72, 29 Vought V-65B, 29 Waco ECG-7, and 27 Waco CPF F-5.

Brazil joins the Allies, 1942

The United States' entry into World War II in December 1941 was followed by a summit conference between all the nations of the Western Hemisphere held in the Brazilian capital, Rio de Janeiro, in January 1942. The US sought an assurance that all the countries of the Americas would break diplomatic relations with Germany, Italy, and Japan, and all but Chile and Argentina committed to the deal. Calming the US military, after lengthy diplomatic negotiations the US State Department arranged for the establishment of US Navy and US Army Air Force bases in northern and northeastern Brazil, at Recife and Natal. Allowing this US presence in the "bulge" of its northeastern region would be Brazil's major contribution to the Allied cause, since it was essential for control of the South Atlantic sealanes, and to provide access to the Allied global transport web. (Even before Pearl Harbor the US had been moving naval forces towards Brazil, and one of its "color" contingency plans had contemplated an invasion and occupation of the major ports on the "bulge".)

The issue of Brazilian participation in the war was finally resolved in August 1942, when the German submarine U-507 (*Korvettenkapitän* Harro Schacht) sank five ships and killed hundreds of seamen off the Brazilian coast. This caused great popular clamor against the Axis, and pressure by the Brazilian foreign minister, the pro-American Oswaldo Aranha, for Brazil to join the Allied war effort. This decision was finally proclaimed on August 22, 1942.

Brazilian–US cooperation in the South Atlantic

The most important factor in the development of strong military relations between Brazil and the United States was the integrated patrol and antisubmarine operations carried out jointly by aero-naval forces in the South Atlantic from mid-1942 onwards. During this period the Brazilian forces began increasingly to be equipped with US materiel supplied through Lend-Lease agreements.

The Navy and Air Force enjoyed priority in this process thanks to their small but useful contributions to the Battle for the Atlantic. The first trickle of armaments coming south included submarine-chasers (SC), and later eight destroyer escorts (DE – one of which, the *Bauru*, is

The US-supplied Brazilian Navy antisubmarine corvette *Cananéia* (C2), photographed in *c*.1943. Here she is dressed overall and her crew man the sides, for entering or leaving harbor. (Courtesy CMG José Lisboa Freire)

preserved as a museum ship in Rio de Janeiro). Brazil also built in Rio three big fleet destroyers to an American design. The Brazilian Air Force began to receive more modern types, including the Curtiss P-36A, Curtiss P-40 and North American B-25 Mitchell, and – to fulfill the urgent need for patrol aircraft – the Lockheed Hudson and Ventura and the long-ranged Consolidated PBY Catalina seaplane. Even so, the main burden of the air and naval war along the Brazilian coast naturally had to be borne by American units. This was especially true in June–July 1943, when a "Blitz" by around a dozen German submarines attacked shipping all along the eastern South American littoral.

During the war the Brazilian Navy lost three ships sunk and 486 men killed (332 of them with the cruiser *Bahia*); 972 sailors and passengers were also lost aboard the 32 Brazilian merchant ships that were attacked by U-boats.

Men of the Expeditionary Division parade in Rio de Janeiro in May 1944. They wear the Type B-1 cotton twill summer combat uniform, the original three-buckle leggings, and the "North American" field equipment. At this date the Mauser rifle was still in use; it would not be taken to Italy. (Agência National)

THE BRAZILIAN EXPEDITIONARY FORCE

Creation of the FEB

Combat and support units of Brazilian 1st Expeditionary Infantry Division
1st, 6th, & 11th Infantry Regiments Each: HQ & HQ Company (comms & intel platoons); Cannon Co (6x M3 105mm howitzer); Antitank Co (9x M1 57mm AT gun); Service Co; Medical Co Rifle battalions (I, II, & III): Each 1st Bn: Heavy Weapons Co (CPP I), 1st, 2nd, & 3rd Rifle Cos Each 2nd Bn: Hvy Wpns Co (CPP II), 4th, 5th, & 6th Rifle Cos Each 3rd Bn: Hvy Wpns Co (CPP III), 7th, 8th, & 9th Rifle Cos *Division artillery:* I, II, & III Bns (each 12x M2 105mm howitzer) IV Bn (12x M1 155mm howitzer) *9th Combat Engineer Bn* *1st Medical Bn* *1st Cavalry Reconnaissance Troop* (13x M8 armored car, 5x M3A1 halftrack, 24x jeep)

The Army leadership had given its approval to the new Brazilian–American alliance on condition that their service, too, was reequipped. Initially they began to receive coastal defense artillery, armored vehicles (M3 Stuart light, M3 Lee medium, later M4 Sherman medium tanks), and some equipment for the embryonic expeditionary force, while Brazilian officers were sent to US Army schools for various kinds of training.

The FEB (*Força Expedicionária Brasileira*, Brazilian Expeditionary Force) was initially conceived by a faction within the Brazilian Army leadership as a means of obtaining further quantities of modern equipment and of acquiring operational experience, so that Brazil could ensure its postwar position as a valid ally of the United States and a partner in the conduct of its policies for the Western Hemisphere. In this calculation, Brazil's inexperienced political leaders overestimated the future dividends of military cooperation. While President Vargas, and the senior Army commanders on whose support his 1937 regime depended, perceived the war simply as a bargaining opportunity, the Allies were far too preoccupied with defeating the totalitarian powers (and later, with the postwar power balance vis-à-vis the Soviet Red Army in Europe) to pay much heed to Brazilian ambitions.

A treaty of military cooperation was signed in 1942, through the establishment of the Joint Brazil–United States Defense Commission (JBUSDC), a body which included a number of Brazilian officers who favored cooperation with the United States in the Allied cause. Some of these officers proposed the idea of raising a large expeditionary corps of one armored and three infantry divisions; in the event, the less ambitious FEB that would be shipped to Europe involved the organization of a single infantry division and various support and service elements. In all, some 26,000 Brazilian personnel would sail for Europe in 1944–45; the great majority were soldiers, but about 500 of them were pilots and ground personnel of the Air Force's 1st Liaison & Observation Squadron (*1ª Esquadrilha de Ligação e Observação*), and 1st Fighter Group (*1ª Grupo de Aviação de Caça*, usually shortened to *1ª Grupo de Caça*. Since this served as a component unit of the USAAF 350th Fighter Group, it is termed 1st Fighter Squadron hereafter in this text.)

An Infantry captain photographed in Rio before shipping out to Italy; he wears the Type C olive-green gabardine service uniform for officers and NCOs, with the *distintivo da FEB* – the "BRASIL" left shoulder shield – in matching material. Note the branch-of-service badges embroidered on his collar. (Julio Zary Collection)

July 29, 1944: NCOs and a junior officer of the 6th Infantry wait to board the USS *General Mann* (AP-112) in Rio de Janeiro harbor. The first echelon were the only troops to ship overseas wearing this old-style Type A lightweight uniform in two shades of olive-green – see Plate A2. In the uncropped photo, "CPP II" stencils on the kitbags identify Heavy Weapons Company, II Battalion. (Agência National)

It was agreed that the Brazilian expeditionary units should be reorganized according to US Tables of Organization and Equipment, and trained in American combat doctrine (the first was successfully achieved – the second less so.) The Expeditionary Infantry Division that formed the bulk of the FEB was raised according to the TOE of July 15, 1943. Its infantry was composed of three regiments; each had conventional support and service companies, and

With some cheerful and some apprehensive faces, this group of men from either the second echelon (1st Infantry) or third echelon (11th Infantry) wait to embark for Italy on US transport ships. They all wear FEB summer twill uniforms and "NA" web gear. At this date variations of the "BRASIL" shield were the only formation insignia worn by Brazilian troops. (Agência National)

three rifle battalions, each with one heavy weapons and three rifle companies. The division artillery had four howitzer battalions (*Grupos de Obuses*) – three with 105mm and one with 155mm howitzers. The standard division-level support and service elements, as found in US formations, included a combat engineer and a medical battalion, a cavalry reconnaissance troop, signal, ordnance and quartermaster companies, and an MP platoon.[1]

Apart from the infantry division, the FEB also included various replacement battalions, which after the division's arrival in Italy remained stationed at Staffoli, near Florence; several rear-area hospitals with medical staff and nurses, two military courts, paymaster and military postal sections, and personnel running a field newspaper and troop entertainments. The quartermaster depots, based around Livorno, were responsible for the division's various logistic needs. (The majority of the rations consumed by the FEB would be of American origin, supplemented with some items shipped from home – the Brazilian troops could not dispense with such popular staple foods as black beans and rice.)

Personnel and training

From the moment Brazil entered the war in mid-1942, the young draftees to the Army were no longer discharged at the expiry of their peacetime term of conscription. Even so, the higher physical and educational standards demanded for the expeditionary units prompted additional conscription drives for 18- to 25-year-olds to complete the newly forming infantry division, which would need its own specialists such as drivers, signal technicians and medical personnel. Although Brazil in the 1940s was a mainly rural society, many draftees to the FEB came from urban backgrounds, and their physical and educational standards were well above what had been the norms for the peacetime army. Most men were conscripted in the southern and southeastern regions of the country, mainly in densely populated cities such as Rio de

---

[1] See Osprey Battle Orders 17: *US Army Infantry Divisions 1942–43*, and BTO 24: *1944–45*

Janeiro, São Paulo, Belo Horizonte, and surrounding areas. Since the Brazilian Army had never been racially segregated, these personnel had the most diverse ethnic origins possible – European, African, Japanese, Brazilian Indian, and many degrees of mixed races – and came from all walks of life. The average Brazilian rifle platoon might include a couple of college students, some former civil service employees and others with a commercial background, together with rural laborers and men from the urban working classes. Although Brazil possessed one of the oldest military academies in the Americas, created early in the 19th century, a large proportion of junior infantry officers were college students from the CPOR, the equivalent to the American ROTC.

At the time the FEB was being raised no US infantry weapons had yet been received; the FEB would ship overseas unarmed, but in the meantime training had to be conducted with the variety of weapons of European origin that were available. The periods of tactical instruction were insufficient, however. This was due to the deficient manner in which French doctrine had been assimilated during the interwar years, throughout an army that suffered from the professional weaknesses inevitable after generations of stagnancy disturbed only by episodes of internal insecurity. Had the French training principles of the 1920s been properly inculcated, the subsequent absorption of American combat tenets would have been easier and quicker.

Once they arrived in Italy, from July 1944, the FEB infantry regiments had to be issued their weapons, vehicles, and signal equipment by the US Fifth Army's Peninsular Base Section. The next step was to put the personnel through remedial training camps set up by the Fifth Army; in practice, however, only the first FEB infantry regiment to arrive – the 6th – had any real opportunity for sound professional instruction and rehearsal before being committed to combat. The 1st and 11th Infantry, arriving in the fall, barely had time to learn the basics of their newly issued US weapons before they were hastily shoved forwards into the Reno river valley in November 1944.

The divisional commander (who doubled as the FEB's commander-in-chief) was Gen João Batista Mascarenhas de Moraes; at 61, he was the oldest Allied divisional commander in the theater – indeed, he was older than his corps, army, army group, and theater commanders. The assistant divisional commander was Gen Euclydes Zenóbio da Costa, and the divisional artillery commander was BrigGen Oswaldo Cordeiro de Farias.

Corporal Antonio and Pvt Aristides of the divisional cavalry reconnaissance troop – *1° Esquadrão de Reconhecimento* – eating a meal atop their M8 Greyhound armored car; note that FEB mess kits were identical to US issue. Antonio (left) wears the olive-green twill shirt and the wool trousers, and Aristides the all-wool uniform. On the glacis plate of the M8 the original white US star is clearly visible beneath the newly applied Southern Cross stencil which identified all FEB vehicles. (Agência National)

ITALY

Initial combat experience, September–October 1944

The main unit of the first echelon of Brazilian troops was 6th Infantry Regiment (Col João de Segadas Viana), which arrived in Italy on July 15, 1944, along with one artillery battalion, one medical and one engineer company, and one platoon from 1st Reconnaissance Troop. The

Into battle, September 1944: a column from 6th Infantry advance towards the front line, wearing FEB wool uniform and web equipment, with blanket rolls – see Plate C3. They carry .30cal M1903 Springfield rifles, US M1943 folding entrenching tools, and most have General Purpose bags with extra ammunition. Fourth from right is a medic, wearing a pistol belt, web yoke and medical bags. (Agência National)

6th Infantry entered the front line on September 15, acting as a Regimental Combat Team under the overall command of Gen Zenóbio. Their primary mission consisted of "combat inoculation" in the area of the Arno river in Tuscany. Ordered to patrol the front lines actively, the Brazilians of 6th Infantry progressively acquired some small-unit experience during about 45 days of skirmishes, company-sized pushes, and minor assaults. At this early stage of the campaign, they suffered their first casualties and took a few dozen prisoners.

In late October, 6th Infantry were shifted to the Serchio river valley southwest of Bologna, where an effort was being carried out in the direction of the village of Castelnuovo di Garfagnana. By October 30, from their departure line in the town of Barga, I/ 6th (1st Bn, 6th Inf Regt) were advancing towards an enemy defensive line held by elements of the German-allied Italian (RSI) 1st Alpini Division "Monterosa." The battalion CO, Maj Gross, was one of the few Brazilian officers with combat experience, having fought in the civil war of 1932. At a cost of light casualties in the ensuing firefights and exchanges of hand grenades, the Brazilian battalion occupied positions taken from the Italian troops; but the next morning the Brazilian lines were hit by a major counter-attack, by elements of the German 232nd Infantry Division and by battalions from the RSI "Monterosa" and 4th Bersaglieri "Italia" divisions.[2] The enemy forced the 3rd Company back from the recently captured terrain, and then moved on against other Brazilian elements. Of these, the Weapons Company and 1st Company of I/ 6th showed more determination. Lieutenant José Gonçalves, a platoon commander with 1st Company, recalls holding his position to the last cartridge. After several hours of close combat, when the .30cal ammunition began to run out, one man approached the platoon leader with an empty rifle, asking for further orders: "Grab it by the barrel and use it as a club!" the lieutenant retorted. Providentially, a salvo of the last three available bazooka rounds at close range stopped the advancing Germans, and 1st Company managed to fall back.

Meanwhile, the remaining FEB regiments had arrived by ship. On October 6, the 6th Infantry were shifted to the Reno river valley to join their sketchily trained countrymen. The *1ª Divisão de Infantaria Expedicionária* (DIE – Expeditionary Infantry Division) was at last united on foreign soil.

---

[2] The 232. Inf-Div was formed in July 1944 from older men and convalescents from the Russian Front. Intended for rear-area duties and sent to the Genoa area, it was nevertheless committed to combat in October 1944, and had been reduced to c.2,600 effectives by February 1945. Its infantry units were 1043rd–1045th Grenadier Regiments.

THE BRAZILIAN DIVISION IN BATTLE

At the beginning of November 1944 the US Fifth Army issued its guidelines for winter operations. Since the storming of the German defensive Arno Line and the western half of the Gothic Line in September–October, Fifth Army had created a northwards bulge in the US front in the Apennine Mountains, around Porretta and Firenzuola south of Bologna. Now its units were ordered basically to consolidate their positions, undertaking only limited actions to improve them. "Consolidating" in difficult mountain terrain and bitter winter weather was easier said than done.

With the arrival of the last FEB units, *General-de-Divisão* Mascarenhas de Moraes assumed overall command of the division, and between November 3 and 7 the Brazilians replaced American troops in the Reno river area. As usual almost throughout the Italian campaign, the Germans controlled the high ground. Among these features was Monte Castello, which was to be attacked four times before the FEB finally took it in February 1945.

Monte Castello, November–December 1944

Some authors consider the first and second attacks against Monte Castello to be one and the same, since they took place sequentially on two days, November 24 and 25. The operation was the responsibility of US Task Force 45, supported by one Brazilian battalion – III/ 6th IR – plus the Recon Troop and some artillery. The attack failed to take the Castello, although another important elevation, Monte Belvedere, was captured (remarkably, by American antiaircraft artillerymen employed as infantry). The Brazilian battalion lost three dead and 30 wounded. The attack revealed Brazilian command deficiencies in reconnaissance, in coordination between Brazilian and American forces, and in the amount of artillery employed. Most of all, however, the attackers underestimated the German defense.

A few days later the Brazilians attacked again, on November 29. The recently arrived units that were employed completely lacked adequate training for the task – I/ 1st and III/ 11th Infantry, with some units from the 6th in a support role, and the III/ 1st Infantry as a reserve. A company of tanks from US 1st Armored Division was in support. On the eve of the attack Germans from the 232nd Division had expelled the Americans from Monte Belvedere; this made the task facing the Brazilians almost impossible, as they would also be receiving fire from their left flank. The result was predictable; the attack failed at the cost of 195 casualties, 157 of these in I/ 1st Infantry. The battalion commander, Maj Olívio Gondim de Uzêda, wrote after the war that he had suggested a different approach, trying to outflank the German positions instead of making a frontal attack, but that he was not listened to by the divisional command. There was no lack of bravery among the inexperienced and ill-prepared Brazilian troops. One soldier almost reached the top of Monte Castello before he was

Reading his mail outside a field position, Pvt Ferdinando Palermo of 1st Rifle Co, 6th Infantry. Note, at left, what seems to be the feed belt of a .50cal M2 heavy machine gun. According to the US TOE of July 1943, each rifle company had three rifle platoons, and a weapons platoon with one .50cal HMG, two .30cal MMGs, three 60mm mortars, and three bazookas. (F. Palermo)

Third Sergeant Newton Lascalea typifies the appearance of the Brazilian infantryman from October 1944 onwards: M1 helmet, US "M41" field jacket over the long-collared FEB wool coat (here with a civilian scarf), FEB wool trousers, and M1938 leggings over low black FEB boots. The *terceiro-sargento* has the "NA" pistol belt, a US M1916 leather holster, and an M3 trench knife with M8 scabbard. (N. Lascalea)

killed; the frozen body of Pvt João Ferreira da Silva would only be found there when the hill was finally captured in February 1945.

That the troops were dangerously "green" was to be demonstrated on the night of December 2/3. Nearly the whole of I/ 11th Infantry, newly installed in frontline positions near Guanella, panicked and fell back when subjected to light German harassing fire. The positions were reoccupied by the hard-working and more experienced III/ 6th Infantry, and two company commanders in the I/ 11th were replaced after this incident. Leonercio Soares, a squad leader in 2nd Company, I/ 11th, described the conduct of one of these officers: the captain "had already transmitted to the major the most terrifying news of enemy advances and uncontained attacks by the German troops. Everything was unbelievable and fantastic; but he ran away, carrying with him the whole 1st Company." This unhappy battalion was nicknamed derisively by other units "Laurindo," in an allusion to lines of a popular samba song of the previous year: "*Quem é que vem descendo o morro?/ É o Laurindo que vem sua turma guiando*" ("Who's that going down the hill?/ It's Laurindo, guiding his gang").

The "consolidation" of the Allied front proceeded early in December with limited operations; further to the east in the British Eighth Army sector, II Polish Corps took Montecchio, and I Canadian Corps took Ravenna and reached the Lamone river.

The Brazilians attempted their last attack of the year against Monte Castello on December 12, but the operation was called off after only five hours. Chilled by rain, the infantry had to attack up bare, denuded slopes through thick mud that hampered the progress of supporting armor, while the overcast skies also hindered air support. These five hours of combat cost the Brazilians 145 casualties – 112 in the 1st Infantry and 33 in the 11th, the latter all in the unfortunate "Laurindo" battalion. Rubem Braga, a Brazilian war correspondent, looked down on Monte Castello from one of the Piper L-4H Grasshopper spotter planes of the FEB's 1st Liaison & Observation Squadron (*1ª ELO*). He noticed that the German-held reverse slopes were covered "by dense pine trees, their dark-green color contrasting with 'our' side, [which was] arid and smooth, where every attack had to be made under the eyes and fire of the enemy ensconced in their fortifications on the top. I asked myself if our men could ever climb that damned mountain one day." Even though Monte Castello was not a major bastion in the German defensive line, their several reverses there made it an obsession for the Brazilians, a powerful symbol that needed to be overcome.

Offensive operations then stopped for much of the rest of the winter, resuming only in February 1945. On December 16 the Allied high command in Italy changed. General Sir Harold Alexander left 15th

Army Group, comprising US Fifth and British Eighth armies, to become Supreme Allied Commander Mediterranean Theater. Army group command was taken over by the US Gen Mark W. Clark, from Fifth Army; the latter passed to Gen Lucian K. Truscott, while Gen Sir Richard McCreery continued in command of Eighth Army.

Holding the line, December 1944–February 1945

However, the pause in offensive operations did not mean that the front was quiet, and the rest of the winter saw intense patrol and raiding activity. A special training program was also devised by US IV Corps officers in order to hone the combat effectiveness of the Brazilians. The inexperienced units would have to learn on the job – and in the second half of December the temperature fell below 20 degrees Celsius. Only a very small number of the Brazilians had ever seen snow in their lives, but they had to adapt quickly. Forty years later, Helio Portocarrero de Castro, who had commanded 7th Company, 6th Infantry, would write of this period:

November 1944: Gen Willis D. Crittenberger, commanding US IV Corps, shakes hands with 3rd Sgt Onofre Aguiar while awarding decorations, including the Silver Star, to members of a patrol from II/ 6th Infantry.

> Our combat positions were too close to the German lines, with a difference: we were in the low terrain, in a situation of inferiority, and the enemy had the high ground, with excellent observation posts. They were extremely vigilant, and didn't forgive the smallest carelessness. Our resupply of ammunition had to be done at night, and even the distribution of the food to be consumed that night and on the morrow. During the day we could only make any movements as individuals – fast, and over short distances.

The Germans also had to be careful, of course, but in their case the major threat was from roving Allied fighter-bombers.

To be in the front line was to be prepared for surprises. Major Olívio Gondim de Uzêda, I/ 1st Infantry, recalls the rare appearance of German tanks near the hamlet of Pietra Colora. His battalion were

(Foreground) Reviewing I/ 6th Inf Regt late in 1944, Gen Mascarenhas de Moraes, commanding general of the FEB and 1st Expeditionary Inf Div; Maj Gross, CO I/ 6th; and Gen Sir Harold Alexander, commanding Allied 15th Army Group. Gross – wearing, like his men, the US field jacket and FEB wool trousers – was one of the few Brazilian officers with previous combat experience, having fought in the civil war of 1932.

A patrol from I/ 11th Infantry pose in theater-made snow camouflage clothing. Their weapons include two Thompson SMGs, an M3 "grease gun," and a BAR. (A. Arello)

relieving men from the divisonal Reconnaissance Troop, who were serving as infantry while the terrain offered no role for their M8 armored cars. Uzêda made arrangements with the commander of the regimental antitank platoon, Lt Paulo Paiva, to bring forward one of his 57mm guns, which entailed using oxen to drag it over the rough terrain by night. The surprise was sprung next morning, when the Panzers appeared to shell the Brazilian positions: "We saw the 57 hit one tank – since then 'Fritz' has curbed his enthusiasm!" wrote Uzêda.

Captain Plinio Pitaluga's Reconnaissance Troop, with only 120 men, were responsible on their own for more than a mile of front line, so they sought the help of two groups of Italian antifascist partisans. Unfortunately these patriots only operated at night, and also gave the impression of being more interested in fighting between themselves – one group were Communists, the other Christian Democrats. When Uzêda's 800-strong battalion replaced the 120 troopers on their sector of the front, he wrote with admiration of the achievement of these "improvised infantry"; Capt Pitaluga remembered this as the greatest compliment he received during the war.

Close-quarter combat by night

The Germans were masters of infiltration tactics, and one Brazilian company had to fight hard at close range to stop one particularly violent night-time attempt. The 8th Company of 6th Infantry were holding positions amid the snow at Affrico when they came under "the most violent coup de main that we suffered in the Reno valley," in the words of the regimental commander. According to one lieutenant who was present, Gerson Machado Pires, the Germans' aim was to blow a bridge over the Marano river. About 60 German *Gebirgsjäger* infiltrated the area being held by the platoon of Lt Ubirajara Dolácio Mendes; one enemy soldier jumped right into the *tenente's* foxhole, and Mendes had to shoot him at point-blank range. Another Brazilian squad were quartered in a church, where they were attacked with hand grenades by Germans who took cover in the cemetery. Lieutenant Pires borrowed a bazooka man from another platoon to deal with them:

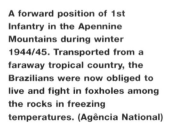

A forward position of 1st Infantry in the Apennine Mountains during winter 1944/45. Transported from a faraway tropical country, the Brazilians were now obliged to live and fight in foxholes among the rocks in freezing temperatures. (Agência National)

When we got close to the cemetery, the bazooka man said to me, "Lieutenant, I need to take a dump." What could I do? He was the bazooka man, so I said "Go ahead." He did, while we waited. Then I pointed out the target to him, and he fired. There were bones flying everywhere, and the Germans left.

The Brazilians also had to learn the risky task of going out on night patrol to try to grab some prisoners. A typical incident involved a squad led by Lt Nestor Corbiniano de Andrade on March 25, 1945. The patrol had a complex arrangement of support elements, including mortars, artillery, and even armor. The squad searched a small group of houses and found German soldiers in two of them; they were able to surprise them without firing a single shot, and so intelligence officers received the gift of four German corporals and four privates from 5. Ko, II Btl/ 1044 Grenadier-Regiment of 232. Infanterie-Division.

The other half of the game was to avoid being surprised oneself, as related by a BAR gunner from 1st Platoon, 1st Company, 6th Infantry. According to Pvt Vicente Gratagliano, on one occasion when they were near Boscaccio his friend Armando Ferreira booby-trapped a gate with grenades and a flare. Around half past midnight, while most of the Brazilians were asleep, a probing group of Germans set off the flare:

As soon as they opened the gate, the thing flashed. The light revealed half a dozen guys, a bunch of Germans all in white coats. I opened fire in a split second... Then I saw another three or four of them close to where Armando and Ferdinando Palermo were. I shot them. Then I saw nothing more.

Armando Ferreira had a close call; afterwards he counted nine bulletholes in the shelter-half with which he had covered his foxhole to keep out the snow. This squad at Boscaccio were commanded by Lt José Gonçalves. The position was large enough to be occupied by 60 men, but after several consecutive nights of German infiltration the first troops stationed there withdrew, and Gonçalves was ordered to hold the position with only 17 men – which he did.

Private Gratagliano was able to use his Browning Automatic Rifle to good effect on several other occasions. On March 5, 1945, when the FEB attacked Monte Soprassasso, he and an ammo-carrier would manage to outflank a German machine-gun position; its crew quickly surrendered when they realized they were being shot at from just 50 yards away. Gratagliano was awarded the US Silver Star, and the Brazilian *Cruz de Combate de 1ª classe* (Combat Cross, 1st Class).

OPERATION "ENCORE"
Monte Castello and La Serra, February 1945

The front got moving again in mid-February 1945, when US IV Corps made a series of preliminary attacks to secure a "springboard" for the final offensive of the war in Italy in April–May. On February 16, IV Corps received the mission to attack a line of heights west of Route 64, a main north–south road that passes through Bologna. This highway, a vital supply line for the forthcoming Allied spring offensive, was under

Men from 6th Co, II/ 6th Infantry prepare to leave for a daylight patrol; note the mixture of Brazilian and US clothing worn in forward positions. The weapons also vary, from a BAR, and M1903 Springfield rifles both with and without grenade-launchers, to an M1 Garand and an M1A1 carbine – not commonly seen in the infantry battalions. (Courtesy Santo Torres – who kneels at the right of this photo)

constant fire from the Germans holding the high ground to the west, including mounts Belvedere, Gorgolesco, Torraccia, and Castello.

The attempt to take these hills was codenamed Operation "Encore." On the Brazilians' left, the main effort would be made by the recently arrived US 10th Mountain Division, seeing its first major combat action. The Brazilians had an important supporting role on the right, which included taking the stubborn Monte Castello. The German positions were strong: they had 97 artillery pieces protecting the line Campiano–Belvedere–Castello, and an after-action report by an officer of the FEB's 1st Infantry pinpointed a total of 42 heavy and light machine-gun nests on Monte Castello alone.

10th Mountain Division made a magnificent attack during the night of February 18/19, when the Americans climbed the impressive heights along Serrasisccia–Campiano, taking the Germans by surprise. They then moved to take the line Belvedere–Gorgolesco, and on February 20 the division began an attack on Monte della Torraccia. That day there was a rare attack in this sector by P-47 Thunderbolts of the 1st Brazilian Fighter Squadron; a component unit of the USAAF 350th Fighter Group, the Brazilian squadron had no direct contact with the FEB, and their operations had mainly occurred over other parts of the front.

The Americans were still fighting for Torraccia when the Brazilians began their attack on Monte Castello at 5.30am on the morning of February 21. After more than 12 hours of fighting, they had advanced a mile and a half from their line of departure, and at 6pm a Brazilian platoon arrived on the crest of the Castello. This time their attack was more professionally orchestrated, by the operations officer on the FEB general staff, LtCol Humberto de Alencar Castello Branco (who would later become President of Brazil after the military coup of 1964). His plan was carried out by Col Aguinaldo Caiado de Castro's 1st Infantry; III/ 1st attacked frontally to pin down the Germans, II/ 1st tried an outflanking movement, while I/ 1st was the reserve. Predictably, the frontal attack was the more difficult one, and called for more artillery support. A few Germans fled, in part when US troops entered the Brazilian sector in error, and 27 were taken prisoner, along with five others by a battalion that supported the attack, the II /11th Infantry. The attack cost the three battalions of the 1st Infantry 103 casualties, of whom 12 were killed.

After Monte Castello, the Brazilians took Monte della Casellina and Bella Vista, and their advance now began to help the 10th Mountain Division, which was still trying to take Monte della Torraccia. This operation was a perfect example of one hand washing the other: the taking of Belvedere by the 10th Mountain had facilitated the Brazilian attacks on February 21, and the taking of the Castello – and, even more importantly, La Serra – helped the Americans take Monte della Torraccia on the 24th. La Serra was taken by a platoon led by 1st Lt Apollo Miguel Rezk, a reserve officer who was the son of Lebanese immigrants to Brazil. Achieving their objective under heavy artillery, mortar, and machine-gun fire, they held it against several German counter-attacks, thus helping to safeguard the 10th Mountain Division's right flank at a delicate moment. The importance of Rezk's achievement was not lost on IV Corps command; previously awarded the Silver Star for his part in the December 12 attack on Monte Castello, he now received the Distinguished Service Cross, to become the FEB's most decorated soldier. His citation reads, in part: "Although in a position vulnerable to fire from surrounding enemy casemates, and despite heavy shell fire and the severity of his wounds, First Lieutenant Rezk resolutely defended La Serra against every fanatical attempt of the Germans to retake the position." Another infantry lieutenant, Moysés Chaon – a career officer of Jewish origin – was also wounded in this action while withstanding determined German counter-attacks; he too was awarded the Silver Star.

Posed photo of a patrol from 1st Infantry. They are armed with M1903 Springfields, the FEB's standard personal weapon; three men per 12-man squad were also issued with rifle-grenade launchers, like this one loaded with an M9A1 antitank grenade.

The gallant effort by the infantry was matched by other units. The division's artillery worked overtime, which meant that the L-4H spotters from *1ª ELO* were kept constantly in the air. At the most intense moments in the battle for the Castello the pilots were ordered to fly much lower – the Brazilian command wanted every single German machine gun and mortar pinpointed for its howitzers. All the pilots took turns over the hated mountain; Air Force 2nd Lt Darci da Rochas Campos recalled, "We were ordered to fly very low… at an altitude of about 700m [2,300ft]. We were actually being used as bait for all sorts of guns. Sometimes the Germans would try a higher-caliber gun, like the 88, and we would see that big black ball of smoke in front of the aircraft." An Army observer flying with the squadron, Lt Elber de Mello Henriques, wrote that "We abandoned the safety limit, and began to adjust fire even against mortars." Constantly in fear of the dominant Allied airpower, the Germans were masters of camouflage. Henriques recalls seeing fire coming from a pile of hay. It was a hidden gun; he noted the co-ordinates and asked for a fire mission, and the gun was suppressed.

The Germans knew the value of the spotter aircraft, and whenever they flew low "the sky darkened with antiaircraft fire." The courage of the men flying the fragile little planes was respected by the infantry. "Every morning we saw the little things fly over us. It was impressive; no matter what the weather, they were there," says Romulo França, a corporal then employed in lobbing 81mm mortar shells on the Castello. França recalls seeing the black puffs of AA fire following the planes; "we thought these were very brave guys to do this sort of thing." In fact, not a single L-4H of *1ª ELO* was shot down during the war.

The taking of Monte Castello was a sort of rite of passage for the division. "Monte Castello was the barrier that stood between the FEB and maturity as a fighting force. Other difficult battles lay ahead, but the fight for self-confidence and for the respect of the American field commanders had been won," wrote American historian Frank McCann in his classic book *The Brazilian–American Alliance, 1937–1945*.

With Monte della Torraccia finally in the hands of 10th Mountain Division, and the Brazilians clearing La Serra, February 25 marked the end of the first phase of the limited IV Corps offensive to the west of

Crew of an M2 105mm howitzer, which equipped three of the division's four artillery battalions. The individual crews had received more effective training than most of the infantrymen, but in the early stages of the campaign the division artillery still suffered from a lack of instruction and practise in infantry/ artillery coordination, which is of paramount importance in mountain fighting. (WW II Veterans Association, São Paulo)

Route 64. The second phase of Operation "Encore" was postponed for a few days because of bad weather, but opened on March 3, again with the 10th Mountain on the left and the Brazilians on the right. It is hard to overstate the importance of the mutual support delivered by the two divisions; as McCann writes, if one of these two divisions had failed then the final offensive would have had to be postponed. But other heights were taken successfully, until the "springboard" was ready. In two days of intense fighting the operation was completed; the FEB passed Castelnuovo and captured positions above Vergato – a healthy change for the Brazilians, who could finally look down from above the enemy.

MONTESE AND THE PO VALLEY
April–May 1945

With the arrival of spring in Italy a new campaign season began, and in April both the US Fifth and British Eighth armies set off; in less than three weeks they would liberate most of the remainder of northern Italy from the Germans. The final offensive was planned to begin with an operation by Eighth Army on April 9, but in fact Commandos had already begun to improve British V Corps' right-flank positions on April 1 by attacks up the narrow spit of land between Lake Commachio and the Adriatic coast. This drew German Tenth Army troops in that direction, diverting attention from their own right wing, where the main British attack would be made across the Senio river each side of Lugo. On April 5 the Americans also staged a diversionary attack to distract the enemy in the far west, where the African American 92nd Infantry Division attacked up the Ligurian coast towards the towns of Massa and La Spezia. While the British offensive on the Allied right continued, the main attack by Fifth Army should have opened on April 12, but it was delayed by bad weather until the 14th.

On that day US IV Corps began its main northwards thrust towards the Po river valley, against German Fourteenth Army positions between the Samoggia and Reno rivers (which ran

February 1945: men of III/ 1st Infantry near Cravullo. Some wear M43 field jacket liners (far left, turned inside out), and the man in the M1 helmet has US-made "tanker overalls." Most wear the US fabric-and-rubber four-clip winter overshoes.

April 12, 1945: two weary members of the 11th Infantry's hand-picked *Pelotão de Choque* or "Close Combat Platoon." The soldier at left displays the "smoking cobra" patch on his "M41" field jacket, and the rifle-grenadier wears the liner for an M43 field jacket, poplin side outwards. (Agência National)

roughly parallel to Route 64). The 10th Mountain Division was in the center of the corps, with the FEB on the left and 1st Armored Division on the right. While the main attack would be carried out by the 10th Mountain and 1st Armored, the FEB would have an important supporting role on the left flank.

April 14 marked the start of the FEB's biggest battle (and the bloodiest fought by Brazilians since the war with Paraguay in 1865–70) – the taking of Montese. For the first time, this objective would call for the commitment of all three of the division's infantry regiments. Even today one can still see bullet-scars on the fountain in a square in Montese which at that time was named Piazza Mussolini; the town subsequently commemorated its liberators by dubbing another square Piazza Brasile.

The mission originally allocated to the FEB was much simpler: to reconnoiter the enemy in front of its positions, and to pursue if the Germans withdrew – basically a diversionary role, like that of the 92nd Division off to the west. However, the potential threat to the left flank of the American advance posed by units of Gen von Senger und Etterlin's XIV Panzer Korps in the region of Montese–Montello was raised by the 10th Mountain's Gen George P. Hays on April 8 during a meeting between IV Corps commander Gen Willis D. Crittenberger and his division commanders. The Brazilian Gen Mascarenhas then suggested that the FEB should protect the left flank of the advance by attacking these enemy elements, thus transforming and considerably expanding his division's role. General Crittenberger wrote in his memoirs that the Brazilians had hoped for an opportunity to participate more actively in the offensive. They did not have to wait much longer: at 12.15pm on April 14, Gen Crittenberger notified the Brazilian division commander that he could start the attack "when he wished" – a decision that shows that American opinions on the capability of the Brazilian division had improved. The FEB would be supported by armor of the US 760th Tank Bn and 849th Tank-Destroyer Battalion.

In the Brazilian sector the main responsibility fell to III/ 11th Infantry in the center of the attack, in the direction Serreto–Paravento–Montello, backed by American armor. On this battalion's left was the 1st Bn of the same regiment (still smarting under the now rather unjust nickname of

Litter-bearers from 1st Medical Battalion. (Left to right:) Pvts Ary and Ramalho, both wearing US field jackets over the FEB wool shirt; Pvt Julio, with a cut-down FEB wool coat – note divisional shoulder patch, and two white overseas service stripes; Pvt Amaro, in a field jacket with the "BRASIL" shield; and Pvt Ricardo, with an unmodified FEB enlisted ranks' wool coat. (Julio do Valle)

"Laurindo"), whose axis of attack passed through Montaurigola and Montese. To the right of these two battalions were the II/ 1st Infantry, linking up with the left flank of the American advance.

During a reconnaissance patrol before the attack the 11th Infantry suffered the loss of a sergeant who had already earned a reputation for almost suicidal bravery. Max Wolff Filho was part of a Close Combat Platoon (*Pelotão de Choque*), recruited from particularly bold patrollers in his battalion, and he had been awarded a Bronze Star a few days before his death. He was killed by a burst of machine-gun fire, shortly after giving an interview to correspondents and letting himself be photographed.

The main attack began at 1.30pm on April 14. While the senior commanders could follow the Brazilian attack from the heights of Sassomolare, which commands a magnificent view of Montese, the view available to the advancing platoons was much more restricted, as recorded by the officer leading the first platoon to enter the town.

Lieutenant Iporan Nunes de Oliveira commanded the 3rd Platoon, 2nd Company, I/ 11th Infantry. Two days before the attack he had made a night reconnaissance patrol that he believes contributed to the subsequent victory. The aim of the patrol was to reconnoiter Montaurigola, a village on his battalion's axis of attack. Iporan had 21 men, of whom three were experts in the delicate task of clearing mines. The patrol departed at 9.00pm from Biccochi, southeast of Montese, and reached Montaurigola without incident. Progressing from east to west across a hill, the patrol then entered a minefield; luckily, heavy rain had uncovered some mines, and the leading scout saw them in time to avoid taking the fatal step. These antipersonnel mines were neutralized in two hours, creating a clear lane 40 yards long by a yard wide. The lead scout who had almost stepped on the mines, José Furtado Leite, then ran out of luck, falling victim to a burst of machine-gun fire from a house on the west side of the hill. The patrol was ordered to pull back, and returned bringing Furtado's body. Having studied the terrain that was to be attacked in two days' time, they had gathered valuable intelligence on the locations of the minefield and the outpost that had opened fire.

On April 14, 2nd Company was responsible for the first attack on Montese, led by the platoons of Lt Iporan Nunes de Oliveira and Lt Ary Rauen. The choice of flanks was decided by tossing a coin; Rauen got the right flank, which would turn out to be the more difficult – his 2nd Platoon were pinned down in front of a minefield, and Rauen was fatally shot in the head.

Iporan had planned to attack Montese by way of the outpost at Montaurigola, but as that had not yet been taken by the 1st Platoon he chose to follow a gulley overgrown with vegetation. Progress was slowed by the need to painstakingly clear booby traps that had been placed on the trail. Then the platoon faced a clamber up the slopes to Montese town; the terrain in fact helped, because, according to Iporan, it "resembled big staircases." His two forward squads were brought to a stop under fire when they reached the top; they were already very close to the Germans, and the ground between them had been cleared, offering no concealment or protection. "Facing these considerations," wrote Iporan, "I did not rush to throw in the 3rd Squad, the only asset that might help us win. I tried to study carefully the terrain and the enemy, and I concluded that if we acted more to the left we

would increase the chances of success, because the 'steps of the staircase' almost reached two houses over there."

Accordingly, he sent his last squad to the left, supported by fire from the other two which were still pinned down. At first everything seemed to go well, but the momentum of the attack dwindled as the squad got closer to the houses, and Iporan went to direct the attack in person:

> The squad was in action, with me in the point position, as it approached the top of the "stairs" about 40 yards from the two houses, and as we were preparing to form for the assault we received an unexpected and surprisingly dense bombardment from our own artillery. This bracketed us, but also the enemy, so I shouted "Forward – to the houses!" The squad hit the enemy positions before the smoke from the shells had dissipated. The Germans remained deep in their shelters while our men overran their well camouflaged positions. Then they tried to react, but were put out of action. I tried immediately to reconnoiter the terrain ahead, but when I did I was machine-gunned from one of the side windows of the big house. I was not hit, but my pants were scorched.

By this rush, Iporan's 3rd Squad managed to penetrate the enemy defenses. The other squads joined in, and began attacking other German positions. At 7pm the 2nd Company commander, Capt Sidney Teixeira Alvares, entered the town with his other platoons, and next morning they methodically began to clear Montese street by street. The postcard image of Montese is its medieval watchtower, which was damaged in the fighting. In 1945 it served as an observation post for German artillery, and Iporan personally captured the two observers stationed there. His description of the scene recalls many a Hollywood war movie. He kicked in the door and rushed in, brandishing his carbine, and was faced from a few steps away by two surprised German soldiers, who surrendered immediately.

What Hollywood less often shows is the effect of war on civilian populations. According to Italian author Walter Bellisi, Montese was the most devastated town in the province of Modena. Of its 1,121 houses,

Mid-April 1945: Greyhounds ready to enter combat, as 1st Recon Troop wait outside Montese for the town to be cleared by the infantry. The nearest M8, named "Teresa," is heavily stowed with the crew's duffle bags and with field-roll packs made with tent halves. The Troop's HQ section and three armored car platoons each had three M8s, with another in the maintenance section; additionally, the scout section of each M8 platoon had six jeeps. (Plinio Pitaluga)

Pvt Olimpio Parcianello with an M3A1 halftrack of 1st Recon Troop. The administrative section had three halftracks, and the maintenance section two more. (O. Parcianello)

833 were destroyed. During the war, it lost 189 men, women, and children killed, and by the end of 1946 the toll of wounded and maimed – including those who trod on German mines still scattered around the fields – had passed 700.

Elsewhere on the same day, April 15, the US II Corps also attacked northwards towards Bologna, on the axis of Route 65 to the right of IV Corps. Beleaguered at various points in their front line, the Germans could now only retreat. By the following day the efforts of the FEB had relieved German pressure on the left flank of the 10th Mountain Division, but on April 16 the capture of Montese was only completed with further support from the hard-working 6th Infantry (commanded since February 23 by Col Nelson de Mello), whose 8th Company suffered losses after entering a minefield. José Orlandino da Costa e Souza of the 6th, who was wounded in the foot and head during this action, recalled: "The artillery bombardment was tremendous; my impression was that the Germans would not stand, but they fought like crazy." The shelling of Montese – from both sides – was among the heaviest of the spring offensive. The three-day battle for Montese cost the FEB another 453 casualties, killed and wounded. The military historian Manoel Thomaz Castello Branco (in April 1945 a regimental signal officer at 1st Infantry) wrote that this was "quite a high rate, though modest compared to the 10th Mountain, which in the first day of operations lost 553 men." Coincidentally, the number of German prisoners taken by the Brazilians at Montese was also 453 men.

(Coincidences do happen. During the capture of the town Lt José Gonçalves – who was at loggerheads with his company commander in I/6th, and had been transferred to his regiment's Cannon Company to serve as a forward observer – was at his observation post in Sassomolare, a little way above that of Gen Mascarenhas. Another Brazilian soldier, Romulo França, was also nearby, watching the town from afar. Gonçalves and Franca met by chance more than 40 years later, at an airport in São Paulo, because they noticed that each was wearing a small veteran's badge of the "smoking cobra" (see below, Uniforms and Equipment: Insignia). It was only 50 years after the battle, when the two traveled to Italy and returned to Sassomolare, that they discovered they had been just a few yards away from one another in April 1945.)

1st Reconnaissance Troop

It was after Montese that Capt Plinio Pitaluga finally got his chance to fulfill the traditional scouting role of cavalry, during a mad rush across northwest Italy. When the spring offensive breached the German defenses and the Wehrmacht started pulling back, the armored cars at last had their chance to run. As Bologna, Modena, Parma, Verona, and other major cities fell into American hands, thousands of German prisoners were taken by the FEB and other Fifth Army units.

The Brazilian division's 1st Reconnaissance Troop now roamed the Italian roads in search of information about the enemy. "He was crazy," several war veterans say admiringly of the troop commander. Pitaluga denies this: "The troop was a weapon that needed open space. Therefore, whenever we had the chance, we went like crazy, and people said that it was crazy. Not so; the troop knew its mission – to take advantage of the space to roam. The infantry couldn't easily understand that cavalry [tactics] have their own special aspects."

The area around Montese was heavily mined, and two of the Recon Troop's Greyhounds were damaged. On one occasion their commander almost lost a hand, and with it the chance to fulfill his long-awaited mission. Half a century after the war one of his hands was still spotted black with burnt explosive as the result of an accident with a Panzerfaust. The main charge of the weapon had been used, but when a curious Engineer lieutenant who accompanied the troop pressed the trigger, the propellant primer exploded inches from Pitaluga. "It was my first real assignment as a cavalryman. I cursed – a stupid accident, just when the war had really started for me!" says Pitaluga. He was lucky; it was only a minor injury.

When Montese fell, 1st Recon Troop had already been waiting in the rear for four days, but not wasting their time; they were studying intelligence on the terrain, the minefields, the strength of the enemy – in short, preparing themselves for the breakout. "At first we had to leave the M8s behind because the roads on the other side were all blocked.... Our first action, from Montese to Panaro, was all done with jeeps. Then the M8s followed through."

The US 1st Armored Division, with strong support from 85th Infantry Division on its right, switched position and passed to the left of the 10th Mountain; the latter was making rapid progress, and on April 18 it swept about 3,000 prisoners into the bag. To reinforce success, the high command directed the divisions in such a way as to ensure the advance of 10th Mountain. There was now a general withdrawal by the Germans right across the Allied fronts; on April 18 the British V Corps profited by their flanking amphibious operations on Lake Commachio to capture Argenta. On the 20th, Fifth Army was already emerging onto the plains of the Po valley, and at the junction with the British front both II Polish Corps and US II Corps troops entered Bologna the following day. On the 22nd the Americans reached Modena, and the British Ferrara; the following day both the 10th Mountain and 1st Armored divisions crossed the Po. On the western flank of the advance, the FEB went on to take Marano and Vignola, and on April 26 the Brazilian division eliminated a pocket of German resistance in Collecchio, southwest of Parma.

After cooperating with US infantry outside Parma, the Reconnaissance Troop were the first on the spot. "I arrived in Collecchio at noon, and I was alone until 6pm," says Capt Pitaluga; "I had already occupied almost half of the town when the infantry arrived." His troop fought their way into Collecchio, dueling with lighter German armored cars; the news of this resistance left the Brazilian command concerned about the fate of Pitaluga's small unit, isolated without infantry support. In accordance with the US Army Tables of Organization and Equipment,

At the end of April 1945, men of 6th Infantry pose with one of the thousands of German prisoners taken at Fornovo di Taro. Most were from Gen Fretter-Pico's 148. Infanterie-Division; after resisting the Allied invasion of southern France from August 1944, this formation fought in northern Italy from late October. A US "tanker" jacket and field jackets are worn with Brazilian wool uniforms. (WW II Veterans Association, São Paulo)

This M8, photographed in June 1945 with its armored skirts removed, bears the white number "19" between the front hatches, and the name "Leão do Norte" (Lion of the North) on the hull side. On the glacis plate is the ringed Southern Cross stencil, above (left) "FEB" and (partly hidden, right) "510" – the Recon Troop's unit code. Other unit codes included 100 (Div HQ), 210C (MP Plat), 310 (1st Inf Regt), 320 (6th Inf Regt), 330 (11th Inf Regt), 610 (9th Engr Bn), and 710 (1st Medic Bn). The officer posing for this snapshot is Lt Solon; he enjoys the peaceful sunshine in clean, pressed off-duty clothing, complete with the stylish black "Natal" boots that became an issue item for FEB officers. (O. Parcianello)

Pitaluga's was the only recon troop in the division, and their armored cars were very vulnerable to tanks, AT guns, and infantry AT weapons. Luckily, "I had superiority in Collecchio against the German cars, which were armed only with 20mm cannons. The M8 is for recon, not combat. It maneuvers well, it's a brave vehicle, and for its time it was good. [The point is] that just one recon troop was not enough for a division. [German divisions] had a battalion with two or three squadrons," says the cavalry captain. Late in the afternoon infantry, from both the 6th and the 11th, arrived in Collecchio to back up the armored cars.

Captain Pitaluga was nearly killed while turning a corner, standing in the turret of his M8; Lt Gerson Machado Pires of the 6th Infantry saw the whole thing. Pitaluga was directing his driver by pressing his feet on the trooper's shoulders: a tap on the left or right shoulder meant "Turn left/ right," and a stamp on both shoulders meant "Stop, quickly." That was what the driver felt as the Greyhound was about to turn out of the main square in Collecchio. Captain Pitaluga: "It was an 88... I had an intuition. I had seen that cannon fire, it had fired two shots. As soon as I stopped I saw [another] flash. The driver even asked, 'Was it you who fired, sir?' – I said, 'No, they did.' The shot knocked through a wall right in front of us. If we had gone another two meters...."

Elsewhere in Collecchio, Lt Jairo Junqueira da Silva, from the 11th Infantry, was placing his 81mm mortars near a church, where German prisoners were being held temporarily. He climbed the church tower in order to regulate the fire of his crews (when he visited the town in 2003, locals showed him the marks of bullets that had been fired at his OP). On this occasion Junqueira witnessed a demonstration of one of the better qualities of Gen Zenóbio, who commanded the infantry of the FEB. In the opinion of many veterans, Zenóbio was no military genius – he lacked refined tactical skills, and had many of the character traits of a martinet. However, his physical courage was undeniable. "That Zenóbio was crazy," says Junqueira. "We were close to the church door, and suddenly Zenóbio appeared, from heaven knows where. It was rather crowded, and I had the mortars in position in front of the church. Suddenly, here comes a German patrol in front of the garden, under cover of the vegetation. They were only a short distance away, and the guys started shooting. The first thing you have to do is hit the dust, but Zenóbio stood there as if he was a squad leader, and began issuing orders – 'Riflemen, here! Sergeant, go there!'... Like everyone else, I was lying down, with that machine gun firing close. But he didn't move, didn't lie down, did nothing of the sort." The general got away with it, and the infiltrating German patrol withdrew.

(continued on page 33)

1: Captain, 4th Infantry Regiment; São Paulo, 1943
2: Corporal, FEB Type A walking-out uniform; Rio de Janeiro, March 1944
3: Chaplain, officer's FEB Type C uniform; Rio de Janeiro, 1944

A

1: Infantry Private, Rio de Janeiro
2: 3rd Sergeant; Rio de Janeiro, May 1944
3: Enlisted ranks' winter uniform; Rio de Janeiro, November 1944

B

1: 2nd Sergeant, 6th Inf Regt; Vada, Italy, August 1944
2: Pvt Francisco de Paula, II Howitzer Bn; September 1944
3: Private, 6th Inf Regt; Serchio Valley, October 1944

C

1: Capt Ernani Ayrosa da Silva, 6th Inf Regt; Barga, October 1944
2: BAR gunner, 1st Inf Regt; Torre di Nerone, November 1944
3: Bazooka gunner, 1st Inf Regt; Monte Castello, February 21, 1945

1

2

3

1: Snow-camouflage clothing, 11th Inf Regt; Bombiana, January 1945
2: Private, 1st Inf Regt; Monte Castello, February 1945
3: Rifle platoon leader, February 1945

1

2

3

E

1: 2nd Lt pilot, 1st Fighter Sqn; Pisa, February 1945
2: 1st Lt observer, 1st Liaison & Observation Sqn; Suviana, February 1945
3: Medic, rifle platoon; Monte Soprassasso, March 1945

1: Stretcher-bearer, 1st Medical Bn; Montese, April 1945
2: Pvt, 9th Combat Engineer Bn; Montese, April 1945
3: 3rd Sgt, MP Company; Fornovo, April 1945

G

1: 2nd Lt, walking-out dress; Florence, March 1945
2: Infantry corporal; São Paulo, Brazil, August 1945
3: Pvt Vicente Gratagliano, 6th Inf Regt; São Paulo, August 1945

The final advance

In the final stage of the war in Italy many Brazilian soldiers rode atop American tanks in hot pursuit of the retreating Germans. Antonio Gomes Linard, a private in 6th Infantry, recalls when a Sherman was struck right beside him by a German Panzerfaust. The tank was only damaged. "The tank gunner was good; he blazed away, and we also poured out a lot of lead," says Linard. "We climbed on a tank and went along. When we were shot at by the Germans, we jumped off and returned fire," recalls another veteran from the same regiment, Paulo Maretti.

The US tanks that helped the Brazilians were usually from 1st Armored Division, but also sometimes from independent battalions. In his memoirs Gen Mark Clark recalled the problem of finding US tankers who could speak Portuguese (or Spanish) so as to be able to communicate with the Brazilians. Modern US armor came as a surprise to the Brazilians, because the few tanks that Brazil had before the war were small, outdated Renault FT-17s and Fiat-Ansaldo CVs. Armor–infantry cooperation, a demanding skill that was vital to a modern army, was only learned "on the job" in Italy.[3]

On April 27 the Americans reached Genoa on the far west of their advance, and the single German division stuck south of the Po below Cremona ceased its resistance; two other divisions were being eliminated in the region south of Route 9, the main highway running northwestwards from Modena through Parma to Piacenza. Secret surrender negotiations were already taking place, and the aim of the Allies was now to prevent the escape of the remnants of Gen von Vietinghoff's Army Group C into Germany and Austria.

On the morning of April 28, Ápio de Freitas, from the 6th Infantry, went along on a recon mission in a jeep with Capt Ernani Ayrosa da Silva and Pvt Hilário Decimo Zanesco. While roaming along in the vanguard of the division they received small arms fire and, as the driver tried to reverse, the jeep hit an antitank mine "and was thrown 30 yards," says Freitas, who was wounded. Zanesco died; the other two Brazilians were captured – but were freed again the following day, when their captors surrendered.

The Reconnaissance Troop were still getting into fights, and at Felegara one of the M8s was destroyed. Captain Pitaluga had ordered one of the armored cars to follow the railroad to circle round the town while he took another direction. "Suddenly a German came running. Over the radio I shouted to [the other armored car] 'Don't enter the village!' When he [did so], a rocket hit the M8 in the engine. It caught fire, but everyone bailed out and we did not lose a single man. They took cover in a ditch, and I gave them covering fire when the Germans tried to get close to them. The M8 was a total loss."

April 28 was the day when Italian antifascist partisans strung up the body of Benito Mussolini in a square in Milan. The following day the FEB received the surrender of two enemy divisional commanders – GenLt Otto Fretter-Pico, of the 148th Infantry Division, and Mario Carloni, of the RSI 4th Bersaglieri Division "Italia." Turin was defenseless and would

---

[3] For details, see Osprey Elite 176: *World War II US Armored Infantry Tactics*

Pvt José Marino, home again with his proud and grateful parents. He wears a cut-down wool shirt over a T-shirt, and cotton twill trousers. On his sleeves can be seen theater-made Fifth Army and divisional shoulder patches, and, just visible on his left cuff, overseas service stripes. On his left breast he displays the Good Conduct and ETO Campaign medal ribbons, and he sports an unofficial medal on his lapel. (J. Marino)

soon be reached by Allied forces, and on April 29 Allied and German representatives signed the unconditional surrender of all German forces in Italy, to come into effect at 1pm on May 2. In their advance towards Fornovo di Taro, just south of Collecchio, the FEB – and especially the 6th Infantry – had to act fast to cut the German retreat, and trucks from the divisional artillery were ordered to carry the infantry to achieve an encirclement. At Fornovo the Brazilians took 14,779 German and Italian prisoners, mostly from the 148th Division. One soldier from the 6th Infantry, Pedro dos Santos, remembers that the Germans surrendered with discipline: "It was beautiful; they saluted, and left their guns by the roadside." His comrade Afonso dos Passos agreed: "They kept their discipline until the very end."

The capture of these prisoners marked the end of major operations by the FEB, although the Brazilians still had the final task of clearing the valley of the Po, where many towns were being liberated by partisans before the arrival of Allied troops. On May 1 – the day the death of Hitler was announced – elements of the FEB arrived in Alessandria, where they met units from the US 92nd "Buffalo" Division arriving from the south. German resistance in Italy ceased the following day; and on May 4, Allied units converging from Italy and Austria met at the Brenner Pass.

* * *

The FEB did not remain in Italy for many months after VE-Day, and the last group of Brazilian soldiers sailed from Naples for home on September 19, 1945. In December that year the Brazilian cemetery at Pistoia held 451 men – 443 from the FEB, and eight aviators from the 1st Fighter Squadron. Subsequently the Brazilian dead were repatriated, to be reburied at the World War II memorial in Rio de Janeiro. The cemetery in Italy still shelters the body of one Brazilian, however; he was found in Montese, years after the war.

The postwar years

After the war most Brazilian veterans returned to the private lives from which they had been conscripted. Early on, they founded associations all over the country, in which they were often joined by Brazilians of Polish origin who had volunteered to join the Polish forces in exile, as well as other émigré veterans, especially Czechs and French. Some of these associations also admitted Navy and Air Force veterans who had not shipped out to Italy but who had taken part in the Battle of the Atlantic. Founded with the main purpose of providing assistance for their wounded comrades who suffered hardships in their return to civilian life, these associations have faded away over time, their marvelous museums being abandoned and their collections dissipated. Nowadays, Brazil has no official policy for the preservation of these museums. This book, therefore, is a first attempt to register the story of the Brazilian fighting men of World War II, as well as a detailed account of what they wore in combat.

THE BRAZILIAN AIR FORCE SQUADRONS

Of the two Brazilian Air Force units sent to Italy, the *1ª Esquadrilha de Ligação e Observação* (1st Liaison & Observation Squadron), commanded by Maj John Affonso Fabricio Belloc, was restricted to operating with the FEB or with Allied artillery units nearby, mainly British. Formed on July 20, 1944, the *1ª ELO* had both Air Force pilots and Army Artillery observers in equal numbers. Training was brief, but although nine of its 11 pilots were reservists they had long experience of flying patrol missions off the Brazilian coast in a motley variety of aircraft. The squadron embarked with the FEB second echelon on September 22, 1944; they arrived at Livorno on October 12, and by the end of that month were at San Rossore, near Pisa, where they received ten Piper L-4H Grasshoppers. They began operations from an airstrip at San Giorgio, near Pistoia, before the end of November. On December 10 they moved to Suviana, and stayed there until March 1945; on March 19 they advanced to Porreta Terme for the spring campaign, and on April 27 to Montecchio Emiglia. In June 1945 the unit was disbanded; its total number of spotter missions was recorded as 683, and two pilots had each flown 70 missions. Although they had been told before embarkation that only one in ten might return alive, in fact the squadron had no losses in action; only two Pipers were damaged in accidents, and they were repaired.

The *1° Grupo de Aviação de Caça* (1st Fighter Squadron) was independent of the Expeditionary Infantry Division, and served widely over the whole northern Italian front. The unit was created on December 8, 1943, under command of *Major-Aviador* (later LtCol) Nero Moura. All the pilots were volunteers, chosen by Maj Moura. Initially there were more candidates than places, but late in the war the unit became understrength due to losses and a failure to provide more trained pilots. The unit establishment was 350 of all ranks.

Their training in American air combat tactics, flying the Curtiss P-40, began in January 1944 at Orlando and Gainesville, Florida. The initial intake was a small group of officers who would lead the squadron and its flights. A second phase of training followed during February and March, still with the P-40, at Albrook Field and Aguadulce, in Panama; during this period one pilot died in an accident. Still another phase began in June, when the pilots went to Suffolk, New York; there the Brazilian aviators were trained on the aircraft they would fly in Europe, the Republic P-47 Thunderbolt. It should be noted that the pilots of the 1st Brazilian Fighter Squadron were different from the normal kind of "rookies"; all had recorded a large number of flying hours in Brazil,

Aspirante-aviador (Officer Cadet Pilot) Joel Clapp of the *1° ELO*, wearing a B-3 flight jacket over his FEB twill uniform, and a seat-pack parachute. He named his Piper L-4H (aircraft number 9) "Luly," after his girlfriend back home, but she would prove unfaithful. (Darci de Campos Collection)

The shirt of the B-1 twill summer combat uniform. This example has three overseas service stripes on the right cuff.

and the group included the two airmen who had sunk the U-199 off the Brazilian coast on June 31, 1943.

In Italy the Brazilian unit would form one of the four squadrons of the USAAF 350th Fighter Group under XXII Tactical Air Command, which had a total of 20 such squadrons. At first installed at Tarquinia, the Brazilians began flying missions on October 31, 1944, at first alongside American squadrons. There was no major threat from Luftwaffe aircraft by that date. The major risk was from antiaircraft artillery, and as early as November 6 the squadron lost its first pilot, John Richardson Cordeiro e Silva, shot down by flak near Bologna. In early December the pilots moved to their new base at Pisa, about 125 miles further north.

There was very little opportunity for air combat, which frustrated many of the pilots. Indeed, the other three squadrons of the 350th Group collectively shot down only 18 German aircraft between October 31 and the end of the war (and 11 of those "kills" were recorded on the same day, emphasizing the rarity of such encounters). The Brazilians accounted for two enemy aircraft destroyed and nine damaged on the ground, but their fighter-bomber missions did a lot of damage. The squadron estimated that they destroyed 1,304 vehicles, 250 rail wagons, 25 bridges, 31 fuel and ammunition depots, and 85 artillery positions.

Overall, the 48 Brazilian pilots who went to Italy and their American liaison officer, Capt John Buyers, flew 2,546 combat sorties. The squadron lost 15 P-47s, with the death of nine pilots – one in training in Italy, and eight in combat. During the final 1945 spring offensive only 22 pilots were available. Even so, between April 6 and 29, the squadron was credited with destroying 36 percent of the fuel depots and 85 percent of the ammunition depots accounted for by the 350th Fighter Group. The Brazilian unit was recommended by the group's commander, Col Ariel W. Nielsen, for a Distinguished Unit Citation (this would be awarded, but only 41 years later, by President Ronald Reagan).

UNIFORMS AND EQUIPMENT

Since the FEB fought under American sponsorship, a misconception that the Brazilians were completely equipped by the US Army has prevailed for decades. However, since an early stage of the negotiations between the members of the Joint Brazil–United States Defense Commission, it had been agreed that the Brazilian troops should arrive in the theater of operations with their complete issue of uniforms, field equipment, and tentage, down to their personal "dog tags."

Given the Brazilian Army's lack of operational experience, and the fact that its occasional deployments of troops had been limited to regional quarreling within its own national borders, the Brazilian Quartermaster board was not as dynamic as those of armies more accustomed to engagements in overseas theaters. Consequently, rather than following an evolutionary pattern of development, Brazilian uniforms and equipment had seen few significant modifications during the decades that preceded World War II, and by the time Brazil entered the conflict the available items were deemed unsuitable for European climatic and terrain conditions.

The advance party of officers who traveled to the MTO were charged with the task of issuing recommendations for the creation of a new series of uniforms that would withstand the rigors of winter combat. Although it is clear that such suggestions were received by the responsible authorities, they do not seem to have resounded particularly loudly. Among the array of uniforms specially designed for the FEB there was a lack of heavier items of Brazilian-made field attire, aggravated by poorly chosen fabrics. In the course of the campaign US Fifth Army QM depots had to issue additional cold-weather items to the Brazilian division in response to the harsh ordeal faced by the men in the front lines.

FEB uniforms

The definitive plan for FEB uniforms was belatedly established on March 20, 1944, to new patterns set by the Army's QM board. Officers and men were strictly forbidden to proceed overseas with items of clothing and equipment that were not included in the regulations created for the Expeditionary Force.

There were four different types of uniforms for officers, and three for enlisted men. These were: the gabardine service uniform ("5th Type C," used by officers and NCOs only); the twill "olive-green uniform" ("5th Type A" – the uniform worn for embarkation by the first echelon of the FEB only); the twill summer combat uniform ("5th Type B-1"); and the wool winter combat uniform ("5th Type B-2"). A twill work coverall was general issue for various other duties such as KP and vehicle maintenance, and there was also a specially devised garment for motorcyclists. Special patterns of uniforms were also created for the FEB nurse detachments – 67 Brazilian nurses would serve in Italy.

The general designation of uniform color was "VO" (standing for *verde oliva*, olive-green), a term that continues to be employed by the Brazilian military to denote various shades. Standardization was never achieved. Officially, there were only two shades of olive-green, simply called "light" and "dark," and summer cotton twill

(Left to right) Lt Massaki Udihara, Pvt Pedro Rodrigues dos Santos, and Lt Irani de Oliveira, all from 6th Infantry; the jeep belonged to Hvy Wpns Co, II Battalion. Udihara wears an "uncut" example of the FEB officer's four-pocket, crotch-length wool coat (see also Plate D1), and Brazilian-made double-buckle boots. Rodrigues has an unmodified wool combat shirt; Lt Oliveira – note helmet stars – sports a rarely seen Brazilian-made officer's overcoat. (P.R. dos Santos)

Example of the cut-down enlisted ranks' wool coat with added breast pockets. This jacket has the Fifth Army patch, and the metal type of divisional shoulder sleeve insignia above three white overseas service stripes.

The trousers of the B-2 wool uniform, with the distinctive front hip pockets.

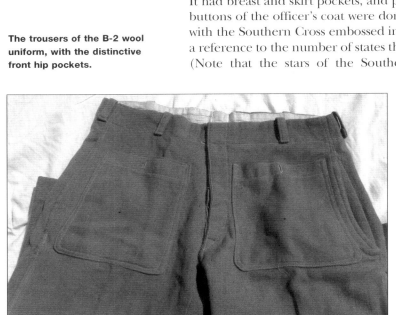

uniforms were made in both these hues. In practice, the twill uniforms could be found in an array of colors, varying from a reed-green resembling that of German lightweight summer uniforms to the grayish shades sometimes found in the US Army's HBT fatigues. The supposedly universal color of the wool uniforms also showed a degree of variation, and original wartime items can be found in anything between deep green and distinctly gray shades, paralleling the many variations of *Feldgrau* seen in original wartime German uniforms.

During the Italian campaign the uniforms most commonly seen were the twill and wool combat uniforms. Both twill and wool combat shirts, worn either hanging loose or tucked inside the trousers, lacked external pockets, having only an internal skirt pocket for a field dressing. The twill shirt was issued to both officer and enlisted ranks. However, the trousers of this B-1 uniform differed, the officer's having two patch pockets on the front of the hips, while the enlisted men's had only slash side pockets. The trousers of the B-2 wool combat uniform were identical for all ranks: straight-legged, with the two frontal patch pockets. The enlisted men received wool combat shirts of a rather heavy fabric, with epaulets. The enlisted men's loose, crotch-length wool coat (in the American usage – i.e. a long uniform jacket) was of similar design to the shirt, but was made of even heavier material; it had longer collar points, no breast pockets, but slash "hand-warmer" side pockets. Troops were also issued sleeved undershirts, T-shirts, various items of underwear, and socks.

With the wool uniform officers wore VO cotton shirts and neckties; later these were adopted for walking-out by many enlisted men. The officer's wool coat/ jacket rather resembled the M43 German *Feldbluse*. It had breast and skirt pockets, and permanently sewn-on epaulettes. The buttons of the officer's coat were domed and made of a black composite, with the Southern Cross embossed in the center surrounded by 21 stars – a reference to the number of states that composed the Brazilian Republic. (Note that the stars of the Southern Cross in Brazilian insignia are arranged in two slanting lines of two and three stars, rather than as a true cross.) Upon noticing the resemblance of their uniforms to German tunics – and perhaps more importantly, envying the smarter and more modern appearance of their allies – many Brazilian officers adopted the habit of customizing their jackets by removing the skirt and the lower pockets, thus producing a version inspired by the British 1937 "battledress blouse" and US 1944 "Ike jacket." This cutting-down of jackets (and combat shirts) was also popular among enlisted men, who used the spare cloth to make breast pockets, and it was officially adopted in the plan of uniforms devised by the divisional HQ in Italy in March 1945.

During the campaign the Brazilians also received a large number of US garments, the most common items being the "M41" or Parsons field jacket, and, during the winter, the M1938 overcoat, the M42 parka, and the zip-front winter combat jacket and bib-front overtrousers – the so-called "tanker" clothing.

The Brazilians received a hat that was an identical copy of the US "Daisy Mae" fatigue hat, but these were very seldom seen overseas. Overseas caps (sidecaps) could be found in both twill and wool, though the twill version was quickly discarded. During the campaign a variant of the wool overseas cap began to be issued; resembling the Italian *bustina*, this had folding rear/side flaps with extensions that could be buttoned over the top or under the chin. Home-knitted balaclavas, US-issue knit "jeep caps" and M43 pile caps were also worn during the winter. Photos also show vehicle drivers wearing a peaked (billed) twill fatigue cap similar to the American HBT M41 type.

Footwear consisted of low black boots for enlisted men and officers, and a copy of the US double-buckle boot was primarily distributed to officers. During winter 1944/45 the Brazilians received large numbers of US fabric and rubber overshoes, which were essential to withstand the rigors of the Apennine winter; however, the US shoepac was never issued to FEB units. Officers also received the low-calf-length "Natal" boot with top and ankle straps – a type of footwear made by artisans from that city that had become popular with US pilots serving in Brazil. Never before considered as having a military utility, this highly practical boot became a part of the FEB uniform thanks to the appreciation by the American pilots of its comfort, protection, and stylish appearance. The FEB "Natal" boot was industrially produced by shoemaking factories in Rio de Janeiro, and was dyed black, as opposed to the original handcrafted boots, which were in natural leather.

Insignia

Officers' rank insignia were embroidered in light gray or white wool on epaulets and overseas caps. Company officer ranks were denoted by a single five-point star for a second lieutenant, two for a first lieutenant, and three for a captain. Field officers displayed slightly larger, ringed stars, in a way that varied from international norms: a major wore one ringed star outside/ahead of two plain company officers' stars; a lieutenant-colonel, two ringed and one plain star; and a colonel, three ringed stars. NCOs wore upwards-pointing chevrons of prewar pattern, officially on both upper sleeves; these were embroidered in blue and white thread on a VO base. In fact the practice of wearing rank distinctions would be almost totally discontinued in combat – much to the chagrin of a number of old-fashioned officers, who believed in rigid differentiation between themselves and enlisted men.

Initially, the Brazilian national insignia, to be worn by all men and women serving overseas, was a simple green twill shield with "BRASIL" machine-embroidered in white cotton thread, the lettering showing a distinctive checkerboard pattern. This type of patch was only manufactured in Brazil, in the hundreds of thousands. Each man

Lieutenant-Colonel Father João Pheeney, chief chaplain to the FEB. His rank – two field officer's stars and one company officer's star – is embroidered on his overseas cap (*gorro sem pala*) and the epaulets of his officer's four-pocket wool coat, and his chaplain's cross on the collar points. In this image dated February 12, 1945, Pheeney is wearing a machine-embroidered "BRASIL" shoulder shield, the commonest type of the *distintivo da FEB* authorized in March 1944.

Lieutenant-General Lucian K. Truscott decorates a Brazilian lieutenant displaying the division's new "smoking cobra" SSI; partly visible behind Truscott is the US Army liaison officer Maj Vernon Walters, who suggested the creation of this patch in December 1944. Most examples were locally purchased from Italian manufacturers in Florence, and slight variations of the patch became widespread in the division during the early months of 1945. (Agência National)

was issued 12 examples, to be applied to the left upper sleeve of all uniform items. There were also gabardine versions of this patch for officers' tunics, and early versions of slightly different designs, examples of all of which might be seen overseas. These variations were always machine-embroidered with solid block-pattern lettering. (While the outline of checkered-lettering patches may vary due to the finishing process, the embroidery was consistent. Any other patches currently offered on the collectors' market which feature a checkered pattern different from the normal mass-produced type, and purporting to be "Italian-made" variants, are usually recent fakes – online buyers should beware.)

Late in 1944, at the suggestion of US liaison officer Maj Vernon Walters and in the interest of boosting morale in the division, the American practice of wearing a divisional "shoulder sleeve insignia" (SSI) was adopted, and a "smoking cobra" patch made in Italy was introduced in the Expeditionary Infantry Division (see Plate C). The inspiration for the design came from a popular wartime quip in Brazil, by which Hitler had supposedly declared that "it would be more likely to see a snake smoking a pipe than a Brazilian fighting in Europe." The patch proved so popular that it began to be worn by non-divisional units as well, which gave rise to rivalry between the frontline and rear-echelon troops. Since the "smoking cobra" was clearly associated with combat, Brazilian infantrymen believed that only frontline troops were entitled to display it.

While the Italian-manufactured patches were hand made, a few Brazilian machine-woven examples were produced in 1945, though it is doubtful that they arrived in Europe before the cessation of hostilities. At the war's end a tin version was procured from a manufacturer located in northern Italy, in an attempt to standardize the design; this screen-printed metal badge was disliked by the troops. The original "BRASIL" shield and the "smoking cobra" SSI were never worn together. (As with the former, fake SSIs purporting to be theater-made examples have reached the collectors' market in recent years.)

During the campaign, officers were allowed to wear the US Fifth Army patch on their right sleeve when out of the line; official permission to follow suit was extended to enlisted men after the cessation of hostilities, but this patch had been worn unofficially by many men before that date.

Some FEB men also displayed up to three horizontal white service stripes on the upper or lower left or right shirt or jacket sleeve (regulations were not strictly enforced), one for each three months of overseas service.

Helmet insignia

Even before the FEB shipped out for Europe it had been agreed by the JBUSDC that its men would receive US M1 helmets upon arrival overseas, and accordingly regulations for helmet insignia were created. One-quarter-size rank insignia were to be displayed on the front of both the helmet liner and the steel shell, though in practice most were only so marked after the end of hostilities. Since the display of helmet insignia in the front lines would have been rather conspicuous, the insignia, initially applied in white paint, were later changed to blue, which was judged less visible from a distance. Original examples can be found in both colors – not all regulations were always strictly enforced.

The 9th Combat Engineer Battalion were allowed to apply a blue "castle" badge to the left side of their helmets. The divisional MP Platoon (which was increased to company strength after arrival in Italy) had a red band painted around their helmets, the Brazilian flag between the "MP" initials on the front, and a Fifth Army badge outlined in white painted on the right side; these insignia were applied to both the steel shells and the liners. The divisional Headquarters Company wore the *1ª DIE* flag painted on the front, and 1st Medical Battalion wore the Red Cross painted on white discs on both front and rear. Other than these, there were no officially recognized helmet insignia. A few original FEB helmets with varying renditions of the "BRASIL" shield or "smoking cobra" patch do exist, but these were only applied by individual soldiers and were never displayed as an official divisional policy. (Such decorated helmets are found in profusion nowadays on the collectors' market, but are almost all postwar fantasies. Apart from rank badges – and the occasional girlfriend's name – no other markings are found on "untouched" FEB helmets.)

Field equipment

By 1942, Brazilian field equipment comprised a mélange of patterns whose designs could be traced to European models of World War I vintage. Unlike the uniforms, many of the available items were satisfactory for service, but in order to give the Brazilians a closer resemblance to other Allied troops it was decided that the FEB should have newly issued field gear based on similar items worn by the US Army. Samples were furnished by the Americans and duplicated by Brazilian factories, most of which were located in São Paulo.

Oddly, rather than copying the improved American designs that were available by 1943, the Brazilian Army decided to base this so-called "NA" equipment (for "North American") on prewar and early World War II examples, such as the US M1928 backpack (haversack). The regulated color of web and canvas items was simply "VO," with no differentiation between lighter and darker hues, and in practice original examples of FEB field gear can be found in an array of shades. These colors can be compared to the variety seen in US field gear between Olive Drab shades No.3 and No.7, and some examples show a grayish cast. Belt buckles differed from the US models; for instance, an FEB pistol belt had the same length and general appearance as a US M36 pistol belt, but with a type of buckle very similar to that of the British Pattern 37 web belt. The rifle ammo belts, too, were almost identical to the US models but

The canteen of the "NA" equipment set in its carrier. The longer neck with a prominent lip is the most obvious difference from the US type.

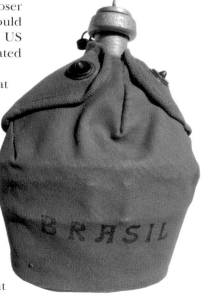

The musette bag of the Brazilian "NA" web equipment. The "BRASIL" marking was seen screen-printed in two distinct typefaces.

with a British-style blackened brass buckle. Canteen carriers, musette bags, and haversack "meatcan" pouches all bore the word "BRASIL" screen-printed in black. These items of equipment were of rather sturdy construction. Although they were returned to Army stocks upon the FEB's return to Brazil, and continued to be used through the 1940s, they are seldom seen in collections or in museums nowadays, and are perhaps the rarest of all items of FEB memorabilia. The following web items were part of the "NA" equipment: pistol belt; rifle ammo belt; BAR ammo belt; suspenders; haversack with extension and meatcan pouch; musette bag; M1 carbine magazine pouch; M1911A1 pistol holster, with integral magazine pouch; M1911A1 magazine pouch; Smith & Wesson .45 revolver holster; canteen with carrier; and first aid pouch. (Brazilian personal hygiene kits were also distributed, in VO web pouches profusely marked with the name of the country of origin.)

Infantrymen and medics received ammo belts, complete haversacks, first aid pouches, and canteens; artillerymen, cavalrymen, and officers of all branches were issued reduced field gear, such as pistol belts, carbine ammo pouches, holsters as appropriate, suspenders, and musette bags.

In spite of the difficulties faced during the organization of the FEB, one cannot say that lessons were learned in terms of the development of up-to-date equipment and uniforms for the postwar Brazilian Army. Very similar patterns to those created during the war continued to be issued as late as the 1980s, the decade which finally saw the demise of the "North American"-type field equipment.

FURTHER READING & SOURCES

Books:
Clark, Gen Mark W., *Calculated Risk* (New York; Harper, 1950)
Mascarenhas de Moraes, J.B., *The BEF by its Commander* (Washington, DC; US Government Printing Office, 1966)
McCann, F.D., *The Brazilian–American Alliance 1937–1945* (Princeton; Princeton University Press, 1972)

Articles:
Bonalume N., Ricardo, "Brazil, 1; U-199, 0 – Brazil's Anti-Submarine War," in *Air Enthusiast* No.56 (1994)
Flores Jr., J. "Jambocks over Italy – Brazilian P-47 Combat Operations 1944–1945," in *Air Enthusiast* Nos.61 & 62 (1996)
Bonalume N., Ricardo, "Ugly Ducklings and the Forgotten Division – Brazilian L-4 Pipers in Italy, 1944–1945," in *Air Enthusiast* Nos.80 & 81 (1999)
Lorch, C., "1st Brazilian Fighter Group," in *Wings of Fame* Vol 16 (1999)
Maximiano, C.C., "Le corps expéditionnaire brésilien en Italie, 1943–45," in *Militaria Magazine* Nos.171 & 173 (Paris; Histoire et Collections, 1999)
McCann, F.D., "Brazil and WWII: the forgotten ally," in *EIAL*, VI, #2, July–December 1995 (http://www.tau.ac.il/eial/VI_2/mccann.htm)

PLATE COMMENTARIES

A1: CAPTAIN, 4th INFANTRY REGIMENT; SÃO PAULO, 1943

In 1934 the khaki uniforms that had been introduced in the first decade of the 20th century were replaced by olive-green, here showing two shades of "VO" – lighter for the body of the tunic, and darker for its facings and the breeches. This *capitão* company commander in full marching order wears the standard pre-World War II service and combat uniform, with corresponding "Mills"-type web equipment, which was manufactured in Brazil based on British designs. His Infantry affiliation is denoted by the hand grenade superimposed on crossed rifles, embroidered in white thread on the collar of his privately tailored tunic. Three white metal stars on his detachable shoulder boards indicate his rank; these have a blue-enameled "Southern Cross" cartouche on the center (field ranks were indicated by stars set on yellow-metal sunbursts). He is armed with a Colt M1911A1 pistol, which Brazil acquired in 1937; note the integral magazine pocket of the Mills-style holster. The Adrian-style helmet is in fact of cork construction, with a dark brown plaited leather chin strap; the oval metal cockade is in the national colors of green, yellow, and blue, with the Southern Cross on the blue center. While this cut of tunic would be kept for overseas use with small modifications to the insignia, the breeches, helmet, boots, and web gear would be replaced, as would the metal rank stars with an embroidered version. The source for this figure is a 1942 edition of *Regulamento de Uniformes do Pessoal do Ecército*, Uniform Regulations for Army Personnel.

A2: CORPORAL, WALKING-OUT UNIFORM; RIO DE JANEIRO, MARCH 1944

This *cabo*, taken from a photo of the FEB first echelon embarking on the American transport USS *General Mann*, wears the M1934 cotton twill tunic with the modifications introduced for the FEB – the "BRASIL" left shoulder shield, and blue rank chevrons on both upper sleeves. He wears cotton twill trousers of a darker olive-green shade than the body of the tunic, loose over typical FEB low black boots with reinforced toecaps. His brown leather belt has a plain brass circular buckle. When the first echelon of the FEB – basically, 6th Infantry Regiment – were shipped overseas, this "Type A" was the uniform worn for both embarkation and arrival. Subsequent echelons would sail wearing the "Type B-1" twill summer combat uniform.

Soldado Otávio Souza wearing a modified wool combat shirt, with chest pockets made from the cut-off skirt section, and showing the "smoking cobra" patch. His wool overseas cap is the first-issue US type. (A. Arello)

A3: FEB CHAPLAIN, OFFICER'S GABARDINE UNIFORM; RIO DE JANEIRO, 1944

Commissioned as a first lieutenant (*primeiro-tenente*), this chaplain from one of the expeditionary infantry battalions wears the "Type C" gabardine officer's uniform, also permitted for senior NCOs. His belt is also made of gabardine, lined on the inside with leather; the officers' darkened brass belt buckle is embossed with a Southern Cross in the center surrounded by coffee and tobacco leaves (Brazil's most common export products by this date). The Christian cross is embroidered on the lapels, and the two white stars of his rank on the epaulets and overseas cap. In all, the FEB had 30 Roman Catholic and 12 Protestant chaplains, reflecting the multinational origins of Brazil's population.

B1: INFANTRY PRIVATE; RIO DE JANEIRO, MARCH 1944

This rifleman undergoing training in Rio wears the basic "Type B-1" twill summer combat uniform, consisting of a light olive-green shirt and trousers, with the Brazilian version of the American "Daisy Mae" fatigue hat. He was photographed prior to the issue of the "North American" web items, so his equipment consists of the prewar "Mills"-type belt with suspenders crossing behind the back, and two sets of four ammo pouches. His circular brass buckle bears the cypher "EUB" (as did the snaps on the ammo pouches) for *Estados Unidos do Brasil*, United States of Brasil – the country's official name. He also wears the FEB three-buckle canvas leggings over black low boots; these Brazilian-made leggings were deemed unsuitable and were not worn in Italy, since US M1938 leggings were issued as soon as the FEB echelons arrived. He is armed with the 7mm M1908 Mauser rifle, which was made in Germany but stamped with the Brazilian coat of arms.

B2: THIRD SERGEANT; RIO DE JANEIRO, MAY 1944

This *terceiro-sargento* wears the one-piece cotton twill work coverall (*sunga*) that was part of the basic issue to every NCO and enlisted man in the FEB; while intended for various non-combat duties, they were sometimes worn in the front lines. They were collarless, with a three-button front, an integral buttoned belt, and a button-through open patch pocket on the front of both hips. He also wears the Brazilian "Daisy Mae" hat with the brim turned upwards, little seen outside training camps after the FEB arrived in Italy. Note the British Pattern 37-style buckle of his "NA" pistol belt; and the "BRASIL" stamp on his musette bag, showing that this US-inspired item was manufactured locally. His leggings are the dark green

43

three-strap model that did not see use in Italy, worn over the usual low black boots.

B3: ENLISTED RANKS' WINTER UNIFORM; RIO DE JANEIRO, NOVEMBER 1944

This image presents a clear example of the unstylish appearance of FEB uniforms. This private (soldado), about to embark for Italy along with the replacement depot battalions, wears the overseas cap, and the loose wool coat of the "Type B-2" uniform over the walking-out tunic (see A2). Almost as soon as men arrived in Italy such coats were often shortened to the waist and the extra material used to add breast pockets, to resemble the British 1937 "battledress blouse" and US 1944 "Ike jacket." Although the wool coats were manufactured from a thick, coarse olive-green wool, they did not suffice to protect the men from the rigors of the Italian winter. In practice, the olive-green wool could be found in a variety of greenish and grayish shades, sometimes dangerously close to the color of German uniforms.

C1: SECOND SERGEANT, 6th INFANTRY REGIMENT; VADA, ITALY, AUGUST 1944

This segundo-sargento platoon sergeant pictured during final instruction in the Vada training area wears the olive-green twill summer combat shirt and trousers (this outfit was nicknamed "Zé Carioca," after the parrot in the Disney cartoon movie The Three Caballeros). He has received the US M1 helmet, M1938 web leggings and M1 carbine from Fifth Army stores since disembarking. The "BRASIL" arm shield is worn on the left sleeve only, above the rank badges which are sewn to both sleeves of his shirt: three blue chevrons, above one white, above one blue, above a white Infantry branch badge. NCO rank badges were sometimes also painted on helmet shells and liners in one-quarter size. His field equipment includes the Brazilian version of the M1928 haversack (which bore the "BRASIL" stamp on the meatcan pouch), and an FEB pistol belt, with M1 carbine magazine pouch and US compass pouch.

C2: PRIVATE FRANCISCO DE PAULA, II HOWITZER BATTALION; ITALY, SEPTEMBER 1944

This gunner – who provides a good image of the average Brazilian soldier in the early fall of 1944 – has jokingly inscribed the shell he is about to load into his 105mm M2 howitzer with the boast A Cobra Está Fumando ("The cobra is smoking") – the retort to Hitler's alleged remark that such a sight would be more likely than to see a Brazilian soldier fighting in Europe. He wears the M1 helmet, FEB wool combat shirt tucked into matching trousers, pistol belt, US leggings and FEB boots.

C3: PRIVATE, 6th INFANTRY REGIMENT; SERCHIO VALLEY, OCTOBER 1944

In this regiment's final phase of employment in the Garfagnana area, I/ 6th Infantry were ordered to make a push towards the town of Castelnuovo. Here, a soldier armed with an M1903A3 Springfield bolt-action rifle – the weapon most commonly issued to Brazilian infantrymen – leaves the assembly area. At this stage of the campaign Brazilians had not yet performed the various later modifications to their uniforms, and their wool combat shirts and coats were simply tucked inside their trousers. (Apart from the fabric weight, the difference between the two garments most easily seen in photographs is the longer and more pronounced collar points on the coat.) Blankets were popularly carried in horseshoe rolls. All his web equipment is of Brazilian manufacture apart from the US General Purpose bag used to carry additional ammunition, and the M1943 entrenching tool hooked to his belt. He wears US leggings over his Brazilian boots, with brown FEB wool socks folded down over them.

Inset: The "smoking cobra" shoulder sleeve insignia, adopted by the 1st Expeditionary Infantry Division during winter 1944/45. These patches were made by a handful of local manufacturers, mostly in Florence, who produced some readily recognizable variations of detail. They also sometimes employed silk and bullion materials for fancy examples specifically for use on walking-out uniforms.

D1: CAPTAIN ERNANI AYROSA DA SILVA, 6th INFANTRY REGIMENT; BARGA, OCTOBER 1944

Captain Ayrosa is seen here wearing the officer's wool coat without any modifications, over a fully buttoned light olive-green twill shirt. Insignia are limited to the three embroidered rank stars on his epaulets and the "BRASIL" shield on his left sleeve. Here in a darker shade of olive-green, the wool combat trousers were common issue to all ranks. He wears the pistol belt and holster of the "North

Soldado **Paulo Maretti of 2nd Co, I/ 6th Infantry, provides a clear view of the unmodified enlisted ranks' wool coat. Note the coat's longer collar points than those of the combat shirt. Maretti is wearing – backwards – the second type of overseas cap, with flaps that buttoned over the top or under the chin. This was developed in Brazil after the initial echelons of the FEB had already shipped overseas, but was subsequently distributed by the QM depot at Livorno. (Agência National)**

American" web equipment, along with a US M3 knife. His boots are the Brazilian-made version of the 1943 US double-buckle boots, known simply as the "combat boot" in the Brazilian Army; unlike the US original, the FEB version had a reinforced toecap. Officers sometimes added rank stars to their helmets, initially painted in white, then changed to blue according to the March 1945 regulations; both colors, however, were to be found on officer-marked helmets throughout the campaign.

D2: BAR GUNNER, 1st INFANTRY REGIMENT; TORRE DI NERONE, NOVEMBER 1944

Following US TOEs, each Brazilian squad of 12 men had one Browning Automatic Rifle. Advancing to occupy positions for his first engagement at the front, this black BAR man wears the American M1938 overcoat, which had to be widely distributed to the FEB in late 1944 to make up for the failure of the Brazilian QM board to provide proper winter clothing; note the contrast with the greener "VO" uniform worn beneath it. He has applied mud to camouflage his M1 helmet, worn over a home-knit wool balaclava for warmth; note also the US fabric-topped four-clip overshoes. His web equipment is part Brazilian-made, such as the canteen and first aid pouch, but the BAR ammo belt is of US manufacture.

D3: BAZOOKA GUNNER, 1st INFANTRY REGIMENT; MONTE CASTELLO, FEBRUARY 21, 1945

This bazooka man from 1st Infantry is of Japanese-Brazilian extraction; he is equipped with an M1A1 rocket launcher, and is also armed for self-defense with an M1911A1 pistol, M3 knife, and Mk II hand grenades. He wears an "M41/Parsons" field jacket over of his Brazilian wool uniform – note the early example of the use of the divisional shoulder patch – along with US M1938 leggings and FEB black boots. This was the most typically representative combination of US and FEB uniform items, worn for most of the campaign in Italy.

E1: SNOW-CAMOUFLAGE CLOTHING, 11th INFANTRY REGIMENT; BOMBIANA, JANUARY 1945

About to leave for a night recon patrol, this soldier from I/11th Infantry wears a loose, non-reversible snow-camouflage suit made by the Brazilian QM depot in Livorno. (The Brazilians also used US M42 snow parkas.) Under it he wears a US "tanker jacket" (properly, "winter combat jacket"), and note the four-buckle overshoes. His weapon is an M1 Thompson .45cal submachine gun.

E2: PRIVATE, 1st INFANTRY REGIMENT; MONTE CASTELLO, FEBRUARY 1945

As from December 1944, much-needed US winter gear arrived in quantity in the regimental depots of the Brazilian division. This soldier belonging to III/ 1st Infantry is seen after the consolidation of positions taken from the enemy on Monte Castello in late February 1945. He wears an M43 pile cap, M43 field-jacket liner worn inside out to expose the pile lining, bib-front winter combat trousers, and four-buckle overshoes.

Cabo Marcello, photographed in March 1945 wearing the US M1 helmet, and an "M41" field jacket with his blue rank chevrons, over the FEB wool uniform – see Plate D3.

E3: RIFLE PLATOON LEADER, FEBRUARY 1945

This platoon leader on patrol can hardly be distinguished from the enlisted men he commands. He wears a US-made "jeep cap," and his shortened Brazilian officer's coat is covered by a US field jacket displaying the "BRASIL" sleeve shield. The magazines of his M3 "grease gun" are taped together, and extra magazines are carried in his front trouser pockets. (The M3 was not standard issue to rifle platoons, but small numbers were available in the HQ sections of rifle companies, and were issued for duties such as patrols.) This *segundo-tenente* is one of many Brazilian officers who opted for US-made double-buckle boots.

F1: SECOND LIEUTENANT PILOT, BRAZILIAN AIR FORCE 1st FIGHTER SQUADRON; PISA, 1945

This figure is based on a photo of *Segundo-tenente-aviador* Alberto Martins Torres, a reserve aviator born in Norfolk, VA, the son of a Brazilian diplomat. On July 31, 1943, while flying a PBY Catalina, he had sunk the German submarine U-199 after it had been damaged by a US Navy PBM Mariner and a Brazilian Air Force Lockheed Hudson. He went on to complete 99 combat missions in Italy – the greatest number recorded by any Brazilian pilot.

Like the FEB, Brazilian airmen wore a mix of US and national clothing, but in the harshest winter period most of their flight gear was of US origin. The B-10 flight jacket was popular, but here a B-3 is worn over Brazilian-made flight overalls, with regular US Army "rough-out" field shoes. Note

Soldado Gabriel Dove, 11th Infantry, wearing a US-issue M43 pile winter cap, and the liner for an M43 field jacket turned pile-side out – see Plate E2. (Courtesy Carlos Scheiffer)

(inset) the "*Senta a Púa*" badge of *1° Grupo de Caça* on the left chest, opposite gold Brazilian pilot's wings. (The badge showed a fighting ostrich – a reference to that bird's ability to eat anything – and the motto meant "Drill it deep!" i.e. "Hit 'em hard!." Torres was probably the only man to include the flak burst in his badge at this date.) At the top of the left sleeve the arc-shaped title shows "BRASIL" in black letters on khaki, edged yellow, edged green. Pilots wore scarves in flight colors; originally the squadron had four flights, later reduced to three by casualties.

F2: FIRST LIEUTENANT OBSERVER, BRAZILIAN AIR FORCE 1st LIAISON & OBSERVATION SQUADRON; SUVIANA, FEBRUARY 1945

This Army Artillery lieutenant, one of the 11 who flew as aerial observers with *1° ELO*, wears a US A-2 flight jacket and US flight overalls, with the harness for the S-5 seat-pack parachute. His overseas cap bears the two stars of his rank. Note the "Natal" boots, with buckled straps at top and instep; originally a civilian item, these became popular among FEB officers due originally to the example of USAAF pilots in Brazil.

F3: MEDIC FROM A RIFLE PLATOON; MONTE SOPRASSASSO, MARCH 1945

Following US Army practice, each rifle platoon in the division had an attached medic to give the wounded immediate first aid. He was also in charge of checking for frostbite and

trench foot, both of which were common during the winter of 1944–45 in the Apennines. Although obscured here by the angle, his helmet bears four red crosses on hand-painted white discs, and a Geneva Convention armband of Brazilian manufacture is pinned to his left sleeve, below the ubiquitous "BRASIL" shield. His wool coat has been shortened, and the material removed has been turned into two breast pockets. Such modifications were originally done by the men themselves, with the aid of Italian seamstresses. In spite of early disapproval by the divisional command, this cutting-down became so popular that it was officially adopted by the entire FEB in March 1945; by then, in an attempt to standardize uniforms, similar modifications were already being produced at the QM depot in Livorno. His wool trousers are standard FEB winter issue with two front pockets, and his footwear are the early all-rubber US four-clip overshoes. His field gear consists of a Brazilian-made pistol belt and canteen, and US medical bags and yoke.

G1: STRETCHER-BEARER, 1st MEDICAL BATTALION; MONTESE, APRIL 1945

This man belongs to one of the nine four-man teams in the Litter (stretcher) Platoon of one of the three Collecting Companies of the divisional medical battalion. He wears a helmet with the Red Cross front and rear only, the wool combat shirt and trousers, US leggings, black Brazilian-made boots, and US Army medical bags and yoke. These companies were extremely active at the taking of Montese in mid-April, during which the Brazilian division suffered nearly 500 casualties.

G2: PRIVATE, 9th COMBAT ENGINEER BATTALION; MONTESE, APRIL 1945

Following US TOEs, the Brazilian division included a combat engineer battalion. During the assault against the town of Montese and adjacent hills, this sapper operates one of the unit's three SCR-625 mine-detectors. His steel helmet is stenciled on the left side with the Engineers' badge, a blue "castle" device (**see inset**). His outer garments are the US-made winter combat jacket and bib-front overtrousers, over the usual Brazilian-made clothing. Men of the division's infantry and other combat units favored such jackets, but they were not always readily available, since rear-echelon troops took first pick of the best items. Though it was not normally seen in the field, this man has sewn a divisional patch to his left upper jacket sleeve.

G3: THIRD SERGEANT, MP COMPANY; FORNOVO, APRIL 1945

The MP platoon for the Brazilian division was originally formed with volunteers from the civilian police force of São Paulo. When the FEB's remaining echelons reached Italy the MP strength was increased to company level, by the addition of men from the replacement depot. The M1 helmet has the MPs' characteristic markings (**see inset**): a red stripe around the back and sides, the US Fifth Army badge on the right side, and the full-color flag of Brazil on the front between the white initials "M P". His winter combat jacket and double-buckle boots are of US manufacture; light gray crossed-pistols branch insignia are sewn to the collar points of his Brazilian wool coat, peeking out from the collar of the

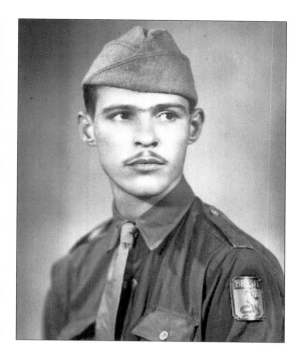

A corporal from 6th Infantry photographed in São Paulo in August 1945 – compare with Plate H2. The yoke effect shows that this twill shirt has, unusually, been modified to the Italian "Sahariana" cut; it is worn with a helmet liner, FEB wool trousers with front pockets, and the "NA" pistol belt and canteen. The *cabo* proudly displays a US Bronze Star and the Brazilian Combat Cross 1st Class. (WWII Veterans Association, São Paulo)

Soldado Aniceto Cavassana, from 11th Infantry's "Close Combat Platoon," in a studio portrait taken after the end of hostilities. For walking-out dress he wears a green cotton necktie and shirt with epaulets – initially for officers and NCOs only, these became general issue during the campaign. The reflection identifies his shoulder patch as the unpopular printed tin version, centrally procured in northern Italy in about May 1945. (A. Arello)

American jacket. The "smoking cobra" patch is worn at his left shoulder, above his blue rank chevrons, and the US-made white-on-dark blue "MP" armband. He is armed with an M1911A1 pistol in a US M1916 leather holster hooked to the Brazilian pistol belt, and an M1 carbine.

H1: SECOND LIEUTENANT, WALKING-OUT DRESS; FLORENCE, MARCH 1945

This *segundo-tenente* platoon leader, off duty in Florence, shows the officer's coat shortened into a waist-length jacket, the wool sidecap, and US double-buckle boots. His rank star is embroidered in white thread both on his epaulets and the left front of his sidecap, and he has just acquired the "smoking cobra" left shoulder patch from a local Italian street vendor. Branch-of-service badges, e.g. the Infantry's crossed rifles and grenade, were sometimes seen embroidered on the coat collar, just as in service dress.

H2: INFANTRY CORPORAL; SÃO PAULO, BRAZIL, AUGUST 1945

The typical appearance of returning FEB veterans during the homecoming parades that were held in summer 1945. Regulations for parades provided for the wear of the helmet liner, twill shirt, wool trousers, and light equipment. This *cabo* has a twill combat shirt recut in the style of a US "Ike

jacket," worn over a lighter cotton shirt. Note his divisional shoulder patch, rank chevrons, and both the ribbon bar and medal of his US Bronze Star; in all, 163 Brazilians received this decoration during World War II. After the war's end enlisted men were also allowed to sew the US Fifth Army patch to their right shoulders, which had been an exclusive privilege of officers before the end of hostilities. Note the corporal's chevrons painted on his helmet liner.

H3: PRIVATE VICENTE GRATAGLIANO, 6th INFANTRY REGIMENT; SÃO PAULO, AUGUST 1945

Vicente Gratagliano (1919–2007), one of the thousands of young Brazilians who were drafted into the FEB, is seen here on the day of his return to his home town. His modified walking-out uniform bears little resemblance to the initial versions provided for the FEB. His olive-green coat has been shortened into a jacket, on which is displayed the ribbon of the Silver Star that he was awarded for actions in January and March 1945, when he was a BAR gunner. The flat black buttons have been replaced with officer-style composite buttons embossed with the Southern Cross. Gratagliano has kept his most intact pair of winter combat trousers for walking-out dress, and wears FEB black boots with US M1938 leggings. His white T-shirt is also visible; such garments, both sleeved and sleeveless, were also issued in brown, olive-green, gray and black. In all, 30 members of the FEB received the Silver Star. As the war approached its end the Brazilians began to receive their own national decorations: the *Cruz de Combate*, 1st and 2nd Classes; the *Medalha de Sangue*, which was awarded to the wounded and to families of those killed in action; and the campaign medal, which was general issue to all ranks. Most Brazilians only received the combat-related decorations several years after the war, as the regular Army was overly restrictive in awarding them to conscripted civilians of enlisted ranks.

INDEX